Living With More Than One Dog

by Carol Cronan

Illustrated by Sue Weir

Living With More Than One Dog
Canine Potenial Publishing / August 1995

Library of Congress Catalog Card Number: 95-92356

ISBN: 0-9646574-0-6

Dedication

To the multiple dog owners

who shared their lives with me.

Your encouragement and information

made this book possible.

Acknowledgement

A number of people helped me along the way to bring this project from idea to the finished project. Charlene Woodward's encouragement and critiquing of the outline and questionnaire to make sure this book would be about living with multiple dogs were invaluable. A special thanks to Carole and Marty Matthews who looked over my proposal and kept me on track.

Once the questionnaires started coming in, it was obvious I could not read all 925 of them myself, so I extend a special thanks to my friends-- Sue Parmelee and Shannon Williams, Shannon's daughter Beth Collins, and my two daughters, Cailyn and Alison McManus--for their help in reading and organizing the information. My husband, John, provided "gentle" editing, suggestions and constant feedback during the project. Without John's expert technical support, I would still be struggling with my computer.

I met the most wonderful people through the questionnaires. I spoke to quite a few on the phone and still get Christmas cards and updates from others. One of those people is Donna Jagodzinski. She challenged my research when needed and encouraged me throughout. Harriet O'Neal, a multiple-dog owner and fellow Whidbey Island resident did the final edit for me. It is Donna and Harriet's expert help with the editing that showed me I have a lot to learn about the English language. Thanks to you both.

When I received a questionnaire from Carol Swindaman, who lives in Redmond, Washington (just a ferry ride away), I called her about the animal behaviorist she used to help with a dog problem she was having. We spoke a few more times on the phone, and Carol mentioned that the veterinarians with whom she works at the Redwood Animal Hospital and Health Center thought the project was exciting and would be happy to do the technical editing for me. A special thank-you goes to Kenneth Jacobsen, D.V.M., Lynn DeBroeck, D.V.M., John Paulson, D.V.M. and Kellee Roberti D.V.M. for their time, knowledge and editing comments.

I would also like to acknowledge my friend Deborah Jones who stuck by me during this entire process. She helped me walk dogs and drive kids when I couldn't get away from the computer. Deborah comforted me as I mourned the deaths of two of my dogs, Belle and Annie, and made me laugh when I was sure I couldn't.

Last but not least thank-you to my parents, Bob and Jan Gannaway, for their support, and from whom I got my love of all animals, and especially dogs.

Contents

PREFACE

The idea to write a book came about while I was attending an
Ian Dunbar seminar. During one of the breaks, the attendees began
sharing ideas about dogs becoming a more integral part of our
lives. I had recently been laid off my full-time job as a technical
writer, and it seemed like a great time to try something new. Dr.
Dunbar encouraged me to call Charlene Woodard, who owns Direct Services, a mail-order dog and cat book catalog. I gave Charlene
a call a few days later and had an inspiring conversation with her.
She shared with me the idea for this book. She told me there were
no books on the market specifically for multiple-dog owners. Since
my family lives with five dogs, I thought, "BINGO, this is exactly
the book that I can write."

I knew how to live with our dogs but felt other multiple dog
owners must also have plenty of ideas and experiences to share.
To get the information I needed I sent a letter-to-the-editor to both
Dog Fancy and Dog World magazines, asking people who lived
with more than one dog to share information with me by sending
for a questionnaire. The response was incredible, and the amount
of information I received was mind boggling. I mailed out 1052
questionnaires and received 928 of them back!

As you read through the book, the issues that are dealt with
will be those directly related to multiple dog households. This is
not a book on how to train your dog, rather a book to help you live
harmoniously with multiple dogs.

I want to thank all the people who shared with me information on their dogs and their lives with them. I have two photo al-
bums filled with the great pictures I received. I enjoy each and
every one of them. The ideas in the returned questionnaires were
so inventive we changed the way we did some things around our
house, and life is much easier because of them. "Why didn't I
think of that?" went through my mind more than once. I hope I
have captured those ideas in this book and you will find some things

that will help you and your dogs. If you are someone who is thinking about becoming a multiple-dog owner, fear not; most folks say
they would never go back to being a one-dog family. This book
will answer many questions you might have about taking another
dog or two into your home. Keep in mind that you are not alone.
There are more multiple dog owners out there than you can imagine.

Carol Cronan
June 5, 1995

Chapter One
UNDERSTANDING THE PACK

To really understand your dog's behavior, you need to understand his ancestry. All dogs, large and small alike, probably evolved from the wolf. The wolf-pack hierarchy is what you must deal with when you own more than one dog. As L. David Mech states in his book *The Way of the Wolf*:

> "Wolves are not just wild dogs. Rather, dogs are domesticated wolves. Wolf behavior has been shaped and molded to make an animal that is more tractable and trainable and easier for humans to live with — to make the dog. In this respect, the dog is essentially a juvenile wolf, dependent on and dominated by its owners who play the role of parents and older pack mates. Nevertheless, the basics of behavior are the same for both animals."

EVOLUTION OF THE DOG

How did the evolution from wolf to dog happen? This information is lost in time, but the likely beginning was this:

As humans began settling into communities thousands of years ago, they most likely had an area that was designated as the community dump. At these dumps wolves would gather and scavenge for a meal when food was hard to find. It didn't take long for the wolves to equate a meal with the presence of humans. As a result, the wolf dens gradually got closer to the humans, making it possible for a lost or abandoned wolf cub to be found.

One cub in particular was found by a little girl who was helping her mother gather berries. The little girl heard the crying of the cub and followed the sound. When she found the tiny, soft bundle, she was compelled to cuddle and carry it around. The maternal instincts of the little girl kicked in, and she hurried home with her cub to prepared a meal and a warm bed for the new acquisition.

When the little girl's parents got home, they found the cub sound asleep with its proud "mother" watching. The father was not interested in a new family member and wanted to disposed of the cub right away. His daughter couldn't imagine her father taking the cub away, so she started to cry. As the tears streamed down her cheeks, she hugged her baby. Her father could not resist the pleading eyes of his daughter, and the pup stayed!

As the young wolf grew, his relationship with the young girl began to change, and the young wolf was attracted to the leadership qualities of the father. The father didn't pay much attention at first as the young wolf starting following him when he went hunting. But, it didn't take the father long to realize that the wolf would be an asset to him during the hunting trips. The tame wolf would hold the game at bay and wait for the hunter to kill the game.

The daughter noticed that the wolf was now her father's companion, and she only saw the wolf when her father was at home. She missed the company of the wolf and wanted one of her own. After a hunting trip the next spring, her father came home not only with meat, but he also had two young cubs that he had found while in the forest. As the daughter was jumping with joy, her mother threw up her hands in dismay. Wouldn't one cub have been enough?

As you can see, things haven't changed much since Stone Age times. Children still bring home puppies; fathers still begrudgingly accept the puppy; and mothers still grimace when the next one arrives. Even thousands of years ago humans had to understand where their tame wolves came from to live successfully with them. Let's look at the structure of a wolf pack and see how it compares with the pack of dogs you might be living with.

THE WOLF PACK

The wolf pack is a family, typically consisting of an alpha male, an alpha female, and their offspring. The alpha male and female pair for life, as a rule, and are normally the only two in the pack to mate. The entire pack takes part in the raising of the pups. Because the alpha female is confined to the den while the pups are very young, the subordinate wolves in the pack bring her food to keep her strength up while she is nursing and providing the pups with warmth.

The wolf pack functions as a unit, with the parent-offspring bond being the glue. These bonds start forming when the pups sleep, feed, play, and wrestle together. As these pups mature and become yearlings, they help care for the next litter. The task of the yearling is to supply food for the pups before they are able to hunt on their own. This might include bringing back part of a rabbit that was killed, or maybe a portion of a kill from a larger prey animal. The subordinates of the pack might also bring back food in their stomachs. The contents of the stomach are regurgitated for the pups back in the den area if the kill site was too far away to bring back pieces. The pups encourage the regurgitation by licking the mouth of the returning pack member.

Order in the wolf pack is maintained through a *pecking order* in which the alphas dominate all others. The domination continues down the ladder until it reaches the lowest-ranking wolf. This unfortunate animal is picked on by all the other members of the pack. In the wild, this wolf may eventually leave the pack. Without its pack, this wolf's chances of survival are slim.

A wolf's position in the pack is strongly related to its age. The oldest wolves are generally the alphas. The oldest offspring will fall next in line, with the yearlings and pups falling into place behind them. In the case of littermates, the hierarchy is determined as they grow and wrestle with each other. The members of the pack are generally offspring of the alpha pair. The two alphas usually work together as leaders; both hunt, care for the pups, and dominate the offspring when necessary to keep order. The alpha male is the leader, although at times, the alpha female may get away with showing less than complete respect for him. She rules the den as far as the pups are concerned.

THE CANINE PACK

The top ranking dogs in a canine family are alphas. The alphas dominate the middle-ranking dogs who, in turn, dominate the lower-ranking dogs. At the end of the pecking order is the *omega* (the last letter in the Greek alphabet and often used to indicate the last in a series). This omega dog is probably the easiest dog to live with because he is easily dominated. However, in some litters the omega would be a terrible choice. It depends on the genetics and temperament of the parents and the environment in which the litter is raised. If one or both of the parents has problems with submissive urination or fear that can be passed on to the pups, the omega from this litter would be the most likely to develop a submissive urination problem, have problems dealing with fear, or even become a fear biter.

To help maintain the alpha position of the top dog, you should support the alpha dog's position in your pack. Many people try to treat each dog equally. Equal treatment is not necessary for dogs. People tend to give dogs human attributes; this is called *anthropomorphism*. Dogs are comfortable with a clear alpha figure. The humans in the family should all be alpha to the dogs in the home. There should also be an alpha dog. If that isn't clear to the dogs, there will be confusion in your pack. It's natural for the alpha dog to receive his food first, take the toys he wants, and always get the ball during retrieving games; this is the privilege of the alpha dog. He has earned that right within the structure of the pack. This doesn't mean the alpha dog in your pack has the right to bully the other dogs; that should not be tolerated. But he deserves the respect that comes with being the alpha. If you try to boost the ego of the *beta* (the second letter in the Greek alphabet or second in position in a particular group) dog's position in the pecking order, he may feel he can take over the alpha position. This can result in a dangerous conflict between the alpha and beta dogs. It might also involve you and require a trip for stitches for dog and owner.

With any group, it is never wise to generalize—canines are no different. It is possible that the group of dogs you live with are all happy to have you as the leader. The amount of conflict in any group of dogs is directly related to the desire of one or more of the dogs to be the alpha and the distaste of another to be considered a subordinate. When you add your second dog, you will have the beginnings of a pack. The more dogs you have, the more you will be dealing with pack hierarchy. Let's say you own four dogs. You may end up with two alphas, a beta, and an omega or with four alphas. You should consider this as you select the dogs that will live with you. That, of course, is easier said than done. As we all know, sometimes the dogs "choose us."

CANINE BODY LANGUAGE

The body language of individual wolves in a wolf pack is an interesting and effective means of communication and often can be related to dog behavior. When the dominant wolf approaches a subordinate, it raises its tail along with its ears and mane, and it may even growl or bare its teeth. Meanwhile, the subordinate wolf diminishes itself; it lowers its tail, body, and ears, and it might even whine. It might also lie down or roll over in submission.

Dog owners must learn to read the body language of their dogs and develop an understanding of what is going on in their pack. The tail, ears, and body posture give you a good idea of what is going on inside your dog's head. These are by no means the only ways dogs communicate with each other and us, but they are key indicators.

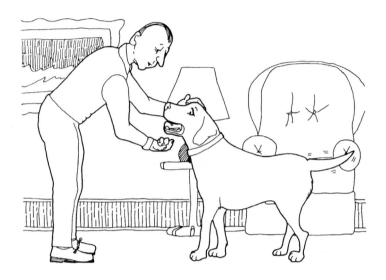

The tail of the dog, if he is lucky enough to still have one, is probably the easiest for humans to decode. A tail that is held up and wagging in a relaxed manner is the tail of a confident dog. If the tail is tucked between the legs, that dog is usually insecure or confused. This is not true of sighthounds; they are bred to normally carry their tails between their legs. When the tail is held up like a flag and possibly moving slightly back and forth, the dog is probably in an aggressive state of mind.

The ears also give us insight into the dog's mind. A dog that has his ears erect and pointing forward is telling you the dog attached to those ears is a confident one. This is either a sign of friendliness or aggressiveness. To determine which it is, you should look at the rest of the body and assess what you see. Is the tail wagging or held up straight? The ears of an anxious dog may appear to be turned down. As fear builds, those same ears may become completely flattened against the back of the dog's head.

Canine communication in dogs that have had their ears and

tails artificially altered by humans can be difficult to read. This alteration includes the practice of docking tails to a breed standard and trimming ears so they will stay erect. Breed standards exist for a purpose, not just for decoration. Dobermans have ears cropped and tails docked to give an opponent less to grab; that's very useful for a guard dog. Likewise, some herding dogs have tails docked to avoid injury by livestock; some sporting dogs have tails docked to avoid becoming entangled in brush or weighed down by mud and ice. (The subject of altering dogs to suit the purposes of humans is a controversial one. It is not my intention to approve or disapprove of the action.) To understand the body language of the altered dog, you need to look at the whole dog.

Most animals, when threatening, make themselves appear larger, and when in a state of appeasement, they make themselves appear smaller. For example, dogs often raise the fur along their back, walk stiff-legged and up on their toes to appear larger. To appear smaller, dogs generally drop theirs ears, head and tail, and often sinks to the ground and rolls onto their back.

If a dog is standing on all fours, holding his head high and his tail and ears erect, and staring directly at his opponent, he is probably revealing a threat posture. When a dog threatens out of fear, his head is lowered, his ears are flattened against his head, and his tail is hanging slightly and possibly waving side to side. This dog is probably afraid and might bite if approached too closely or cornered.

On the other hand, if the dog has the front half of his body lowered with his front legs on the ground and has his rump in the air with tail wagging, you have just witnessed a play bow. This dog is saying, "Come on, let's have some fun."

The submissive posture for a dog is very similar to the way subordinate wolves act with the alphas in their pack. The dog will get low to the ground with his ears flat against his head and his tail between his legs, and he may wag his rear end back and forth. You might even see the dog lick the other dog around the muzzle. This is similar to the way wolf pups lick the mouths of the pack mates that return to the den with a stomach full of food to feed them.

Remember, wolf pups are at the lowest end of the pecking order in a wolf pack. In an extreme case of submissiveness, the groveling dog may even urinate. This shows respect to the dog being greeted.

You may even be dealing with this show of respect in your home. You, the human alpha, are greeting your dog after a day at the office. The dog gets low and right in front of you urinates on the floor. Some owners may look at this as a deliberate sign of disobedience and reprimand the dog. In actuality this will only make the situation worse, because now the dog will attempt to be even more submissive. To break the cycle you might try ignoring your dog for a few minutes, then getting on the same level as your dog, and saying your hellos in a calm manner.

YOU, THE PACK LEADER

Does any of this information apply to your pack of dogs? If it does, you're probably already able to understand the communication that exists with wolves and dogs. As a dog owner, you must maintain the role of leader, or alpha. This is true if you own one dog or many. If you're not the leader, you're in for some trouble! Chaos will reign supreme.

Your role as alpha must remain untouchable. The best way to maintain this is through training. Each dog should respond to basic obedience commands, and house rules must be set and followed. A regular routine is invaluable in keeping things going smoothly around the house. Of course, each dog and pack of dogs is different, and because of that individuality there is no set of rules that works in all situations. In Chapter 2, "Room for One More," we look at some of the problems of adding new members to your pack, and the fun that can result from a successful introduction.

If you have a basic understanding of the wolf and its pack structure, you can deal with your dog's behavior in a way your dog will understand.

SUGGESTED READING

Dunbar, Ian. *Dog Behavior.* T.F.H. Publications Inc., Neptune, NJ. 1979

Fox, M.W. *Understanding Your Dog.* Coward, McCann and Geoghegan, Inc., New York, NY. 1972

Mech, L.D. *The Way of the Wolf.* Voyageur Press, MN. 1991

Chapter Two
ROOM FOR ONE MORE

With 15 million unwanted dogs being killed each year, it is easy to see why you might come to own more than one dog. It's not hard to find dogs that need homes! In this chapter, we will look at the process of building a canine pack and examine some ideas that might make the transition smoother for everyone involved.

Most dog owners work outside the home to pay the rent, vet bills, food bills for dogs and humans—the general necessities of life. This does not mean it is impossible to own more than one dog, but it may take a little more planning. To start with, it is a good idea to take a few days off of work when you get your new dog or puppy to help with the adjustment period. It's best if you can plan on taking some vacation time, but if that's not possible, at least try to bring the new family member home just prior to a weekend.

Once you own two dogs, you are on your way to living with a pack of dogs, but the dynamics of a pack often do not begin to form until you add a third dog. The following situation illustrates this point.

TWO'S COMPANY

Suppose you have two German Shepherd Dogs (GSDs) that get along great together. The two puppies are litter mates, but you got them at different times. Both have gone through obedience training, and it has been fun watching them grow and mature. A short time later, you make a new friend at the German Shepherd Club that breeds both GSDs and Shetland Sheepdogs, or "Shelties." One of her Shelties just had a litter of very cute puppies. (You can see it coming, can't you?) The breeder was planning on keeping one of the males. Unfortunately, by the age of six months, the male the breeder kept is too big to be shown in AKC conformation dog shows, but he would make a great obedience dog. (In a conformation show the dog is judged against the breed standard, which states a Sheltie needs to be between 13 and 16 inches tall; he is already 19 inches.) Your friend has seen what a great job you have done with the GSDs in obedience and wonders if you would be interested in welcoming this Sheltie, named Bayou, into your home.

This is exactly what happened to Linda and Richard. When they first brought Bayou home, the GSDs, Carrie and Justin, were a little surprised that their territory was being invaded. The initial introduction was held outside of the home, one dog at a time, on leash, with Bayou staying in his wire crate in the car. Both of the Shepherds reacted aggressively, which made Bayou react timidly. Carrie and Justin were encouraged to calm down through the use of some of their obedience training, and a *jolly routine* was used for Bayou to help alleviate the timid feelings. A jolly routine can be described as letting your dog know that there is nothing to be afraid of in a laughing, jolly manner.

As you can see from this scenario, it was going to be a while before things would be "back to normal" at Linda and Richard's house. Certainly, some introductions go as smooth as silk, and the new and old dog are playing together like old friends by evening, but don't count on it! This is where doing your homework prepares you for anything that might happen. Before you ever bring the new dog into your house, you need to make a *commitment* to yourself and to the new member of your canine family that you will try everything you can to make it work.

Let's get back to Carrie, Justin, and Bayou. When the situation calmed down later that day, Bayou was put in his crate in the master bedroom. Justin and Carrie could then sniff the newcomer through the door but not see him to intimidate him. As the two GSDs became more accustomed to the smell of Bayou in their domain, it became time to take the introduction one step farther.

Two days later, Justin and Carrie were brought, one at a time, into the bedroom on leash to sniff Bayou, still in the crate. At this point any further signs of aggression were firmly corrected. About one week after Bayou was brought into his new home, it was time for nose-to-nose introductions—first, one at a time, and then all three together. After a successful three-nose introduction, Linda and Richard knew the end was in sight. Finally, the dogs were allowed supervised time together with all three dogs off leash. It was a lengthy process. Altogether, it took about three weeks, but they all survived with no vet bills. Now all three dogs are pals, so it was worth the effort.

THE POWER OF COMMITMENT

Another couple, Charlene and Glenn, have also been put to the test. Once again, a commitment to making the situation work out was critical. In this case, Glenn and Charlene had six dogs that, for the most part, got along. The problem was with two females, one a spayed Doberman Pinscher, Sasha, and the other a spayed Shiloh Shepherd, Nicky. Sasha was 1 year old, and Nicky was about 18 months old when she was found and taken into the pack. Having experienced the introductions of many dogs into their multi-dog household, the method that works for Charlene and Glenn is to keep the new dog with them constantly on leash for the first month while he or she is integrated into the pack. The leash is a quick and effective tool to break up any canine confrontations. It also helps ensure the dog is always available for praise and reprimands. In this case, Nicky needed to be on leash for four months, just to be sure she would not jump the fence, as she was half-wild when they found her.

Fence jumping was not the only problem.The problem that would take the most dedication and commitment was that Sasha could not stand the sight of Nicky and would attack her at the least provocation Sasha absolutely wanted to drive Nicky out of the pack. As a result, there were fights and continual confrontations. This behavior seemed to be more severe while the dogs were out in the yard. Charlene noticed that Sasha was constantly watching for a reason to chase Nicky, and when Sasha caught Nicky, Sasha would attack and Nicky would yelp. This was the fuel for the fire that kept Sasha always ready to initiate a fight. During the fight, Sasha usually ended up with the bruises. Nicky had a very thick coat that protected her from Sasha's teeth. Since Sasha was always the instigator in the confrontations, Charlene and Glenn began keeping her on leash. The dogs were kept in separate rooms when they could not be supervised.

To help the dogs deal with their differences, Charlene would put Sasha in a down-stay and have Nicky face her in a sit-stay. This reminds me of how my Mom handled fights between my brothers and sister and me. We had to sit in chairs facing each other for a given amount of time; most of the time we would end up laughing. I don't think the dogs ever laughed, but they did learn to tolerate each other. This went on for three years until the dogs reached the point where they could be together in the house, the yard, or even during a ride in the car; however, they were never reliable enough to be left alone unsupervised. During the last year these two dogs lived together, Sasha was diagnosed with pancreatic cancer and was euthanized for health reasons. The other dogs in the family pack were not involved directly in the fights and managed to leave the problem between Sasha and Nicky.

This dramatic example of commitment is best described by Charlene herself. "I had made up my mind that I would do whatever it took to keep us all together." To that end, I believe this family found success, and the experience of dealing with these two dogs has left them with an invaluable knowledge of dog behavior.

WHEN YOU'RE THE WRONG FAMILY

This next story has a different ending than the story about Charlene and Glenn's canine family, although the basis of it is the same: two dogs that did not get along.

Anne owned three Cocker Spaniels, two females and a male, and was very involved in Cocker Spaniel Rescue of Greater Boston. Eighty percent of the dogs rescued by Cocker Spaniel Rescue are from families who can no longer manage to keep their dog.

Blackie came into Anne's life through a phone call to Cocker Spaniel Rescue. He had lived his first five years in an outdoor pen, as an outdoor dog that was not a part of a family. When Blackie came to Anne's house as a foster dog, he had no manners and was jumping on counters and flying over the furniture. Anne had her work cut out as the foster "mother."

As Anne introduced Blackie to Hillie, Cokie, and Bandit (all of the dogs are Cocker Spaniels and spayed or neutered), it was apparent that Blackie and Bandit (both males) were not going to get along. They fought immediately, with the initial confrontation drawing blood. From then on Anne had to keep them separated. During the next year Anne learned a lot about dog behavior; she talked to behaviorists and read many books. She took both dogs to training classes so they could learn to be together outside and inside the house.

Anne felt she had done everything to make it work between Blackie and Bandit, but she finally came to the conclusion that she couldn't force these two dogs to live together; it was not going to happen. With tears in her eyes, she called the newspaper and placed an ad. The response to an ad for a 5-year-old dog was light, but one special family called, and Anne decided to go and meet them.

She loaded Blackie in the car with his things, just in case it was the right home. Anne had a feeling it was going to be because she was so impressed by their phone conversation. The prospective family had one very old female dog and was willing to work with Blackie on his manners. Since the older dog was not a threat to Blackie, it worked out fine. The connection was made, and

Blackie at last found his perfect home.

In hindsight, Anne felt she could have handled the whole situation better if she had admitted to herself sooner that it was not going to work. She feels she didn't make that decision because she let her personal feelings get in the way. She loved Blackie and wanted him to be a part of her family. When she finally resolved to place him in a new home with no other dogs, she found that Blackie was much happier than he ever could have been in her multiple-dog household.

In the next story you'll see how we wish all introductions would go.

LITTLE ORPHANED ANNIE

Tom's dog, Paddywack, had died of cancer, leaving Cricket, a 6-year-old West Highland White Terrier, as an only dog. Since Cricket was Donna's (Tom's wife) dog, Tom began a two year search for the dog that would be just right. His search finally came to an end when he came across 3-month-old Annie, a Lhasa Apso/Dachshund mix puppy at a shelter near his work. Another person was also interested in Annie, so Tom felt it was destiny that he was able to bring her home. This union took place during Tom's lunch hour, causing Annie to spend half of a day at his office. During Tom's time at work, Annie received goodies and milk from all those people who cannot help giving a puppy something to eat. Subsequently, during the drive home in rush-hour traffic, she got carsick. The first order of business when they arrived home was to clean up Annie (and Tom). Donna did the honors of bathing Annie, while Tom attended to the car and himself. It was soon after Annie was clean and smelling fine that she met her new sister, Cricket. In an hour, they were getting along fine.

Donna and Tom have enjoyed their two dogs so much that two years later they added a third dog to their pack, a 3-month-old male Cairn Terrier that Donna saw and couldn't get off her mind. Since Duffy was accustomed to being with other dogs at his other home, this introduction went even better than the first. Tom and

Donna brought Cricket and Annie out into the front yard to meet Duffy, and immediately the two girls fell in love with him.

The families described here are good examples of the fact that anything can happen when you introduce a new dog or puppy into an already established pack. There are some basic ground rules for introducing newcomers into your home. These are proven methods that have worked for others. Since you know your dogs the best, it is up to you to decide which would work best for you and your dogs.

THE NEW PUPPY

A puppy is usually the easiest to introduce to an established pack. You should always closely supervise any introduction. Following the introduction, there is usually a probation period before you can leave the dogs together unsupervised. One month is a good estimate of the time it might take, though this can vary considerably. In most cases, the new dog is introduced and all is well in a few days.

Some adult dogs might just ignore the new puppy and look at you like you have lost your mind bringing "it" into their house. Others might start licking and nurturing it right away. When introducing puppies, keep in mind that some pups lack respect and are too playful for middle-aged or older dogs. Once the puppy is crate-trained (more on crate training in Chapter Five), the established dogs can get used to the rowdy pup while he is in the crate without him jumping all over them.

THE NEW ADULT

The safest and most common place to introduce the new dog is on neutral territory: a local park, the neighbor's yard, or at the shelter where you are getting the dog. This is generally done while watching both dogs carefully, preferably while they are on a loose leash. Allow the dogs to sniff each other. If this goes well, you can then put the dogs in a fenced area, with leashes dragging, and al low them to continue getting to know each other.

Another introduction variation is having the new dog meet its new family in their backyard. One method is to give treats to all the dogs so they will think getting a new brother or sister is a good thing. The food may also be a good distraction for the established dogs; they will concentrate more on the food and less on the newcomer. This method can be risky if you have food issues you must deal with during mealtime with the dogs you have already.

The use of a crate, like Linda and Richard did when introducing their dogs, can make introductions go smoothly. First, place the new dog in his crate, inside the house. Then, allow the other dogs in, one at a time, to sniff the newcomer through the crate. Next, turn the tables and place the established dogs in crates and let the new one sniff them while they are in the crates.

You should now have a pretty good idea of which dogs will get along with the newcomer and which may need more incentive. If one of your dogs doesn't get along with the new dog, take the dogs that need more time to adjust to each other away from the home environment, and do an activity that the dogs will enjoy together. A walk on leash may be all it takes. You might branch out and do some obedience work, or take a ride in the car with the new dog in a crate—anything that will help create a bond between the dogs.

If you don't use crates or don't have enough crates for all of your dogs, you can always use baby gates to restrict the new dog to a certain area. With baby gates, the dogs will be able to sniff without the restrictions of the crate. You can also gauge the level of interest the established dogs have in the newcomer, because once they are used to the new dog's smell, they will probably just walk away from the gate and find something else to do. The new dog will also be able to get to his water dish and explore his new surroundings without the interference of the other dogs.

If you have outdoor dogs, you might find it necessary to put up a temporary fence to divide your yard. This will help if the initial introductions don't go smoothly and you need more than a few days to get things worked out. If you have dog kennels in your yard, you can separate the dogs in the kennels and let them sniff each other through the fencing. After the dogs are accustomed to each other, they should be allowed to play together for 10 or 15 minutes a day, under supervision. If all goes well, you should be able to leave them together in a week or two.

WHEN INTRODUCTIONS DON'T GO ACCORDING TO PLAN

Remember, most dogs will eventually get to be friends. If you have given the new dog a reasonable period of time to become acclimated and he still hasn't adjusted, you will need to look at your alternatives. You may discover that the extra fence you put up in your backyard must be left up permanently. Or, you may have to keep the dogs in separate rooms and never allow those that won't get along to be together.

In some families, there are only two dogs that won't get along. If that is the case, these two dogs can be rotated in and out of a room used to separate them (an *isolation room*). This has the advantage of giving the isolated dog some time alone, and it can save you money in vet bills. To make it a special place to go, you can equip the isolation room with special toys and a nice bed.

If you have five or more dogs, you could end up having two separate packs. Some people work this out by having an outside group of dogs and an indoor group of dogs. Especially if all of your dogs don't get along, you might need to maintain two separate yards: one for the dogs that live outside and one for the indoor dogs to use for eliminating and exercise. This will work if you make a point of spending time with each group. The indoor dogs will be around you more, but if you set aside time each day to spend socializing with the outdoor dogs, they will not feel neglected. They do, after all, have each other.

When you have an established pack, and you have taken the time to understand what is going on in that pack, you will be able to decide what type of dog will work out best in your group. Quite a few people who responded to my questionnaire made it clear they would only introduce puppies into their packs. The few times they tried introducing adult dogs, it did not work out. For them, the amount of disruption in the established pack wasn't worth it, and a puppy caused the least amount of stress. Other packs whose humans like to rescue dogs of all ages are accustomed to new dogs coming into their homes and will not even notice when one doesn't eventually leave. Each dog and group of dogs is individual, and you should assess yours with honesty, not emotion.

The solutions mentioned so far have all involved physical barriers—crates, baby gates, isolation rooms, kennels, or dividing the yard. If these solutions are not practical for you, the use of behavior modification or training may be the solution.

Behavior Modification and Training

Generally, people give away or abandon an adult dog because of behavior problems. These problems can be simple (like pulling on leash or house soiling) or complex (like aggression problems) in nature. Starting the newcomer in an obedience class or following the lessons in one of the many training books available is a good first step. Training goes a long way in getting control of a situation. You may need to call a behavior consultant or your vet, or read up on behavior problems to find a solution to your specific problem. A list of recommended reading is presented at the end of this chapter. In Chapter 3 we will discuss the criteria needed to select a trainer or a behavior consultant.

Now let's look at your options when you can't make it work out between the dogs you already own and the newcomer.

WHEN THE NEW DOG JUST DOESN'T FIT IN

We have already talked about *commitment* being the key to making it work. Some people will make it work no matter what. You must take an honest look at the situation to decide if you have truly used all the avenues open to you.

At this point, let's say you have tried everything, and it is just not going to work out for you. Your commitment at this point should be to find a new home for the dog that is causing the disruption. Since it takes two dog to cause a conflict, you will have to decide if it is the newcomer that should be placed or the other dog. You must be sure you are not just passing your problem off to some other unsuspecting soul. If the dog is aggressive, psychotic, or in some way unfit to be placed in a new home, it is up to you to have that dog euthanized. This decision should be made if you have tried all of the above suggestions, training has not worked, and in your heart you feel that the dog is unsafe. This is a very hard decision to make, but it is the humane way to handle a dog of this type.

However, if the dog has not worked out because of the multiple-dog environment in your home, you should be able to find a home that doesn't yet have a dog. You can do this through word-of-mouth, rescue organizations, obedience clubs, kennel clubs, or even a word to your vet. An ad in the newspaper can be risky unless you have an intense screening procedure. If this is the way you decide to go, make sure you have questions prepared before hand, and don't be afraid to say "no" to anyone who does not offer the kind of home you feel your dog needs. You can get a good idea of the questions to ask at your local humane animal shelter. Quite a few of these organizations require prospective dog owners to fill out very detailed questionnaires before the organization will release an animal to them. See the accompanying screening procedure used by the Cocker Spaniel Rescue of Greater Boston (modified slightly for our purposes) for an outline you can follow to make sure the dog in your care will find a good permanent home.

1. Have you ever owned a dog before?
2. List the dogs you have owned (as an adult) including:
   - Dates of ownership
   - Breed
   - Male or female
   - Spayed or neutered
   - Date of death or when given up
3. If you elected to give up your dog, please explain the reason and give the location of dog now.
4. Do you rent or own your apartment or house?
   Please provide landlord's name, address, and phone number for consent to have a dog on the property.
5. How long have you lived at the above address? If you move, will you take your dog with you?
6. Do you have a fenced yard? State height of fence and type of fencing.
7. If you don't have a fenced yard, are you planning to have a fence installed before you adopt a dog?
8. Knowing that all dogs tend to roam, are you willing to protect your dog from injury, theft, or death by always containing the dog in a fenced area or run, in the house, or with you on a leash?
9. Will your dog come into contact with children?
   - If so, where.
10. Does anyone in your family have pet allergies? Please explain.

11. What are the work schedules of adults in the household?
12. Is anyone home during the day?
13. Where will the dog be left when you are out?
14. Where will the dog sleep?
15. Please describe the perfect dog for you. Think about your lifestyle: are you active, in and out a lot, with lots of people/ friends around or are you sedentary, quiet, relaxed, with few visitors? Would a dog go with you everywhere or would you be more inclined to leave it home?
16. How do you feel about obedience school? Have you ever trained a dog before?
17. What is your expectation regarding an adopted dog's level of training?
    • Very reliable at obeying verbal commands such as; sit, down, stay, or heel?
    • Walking nicely on a leash and not jumping on visitors.
    • Not going potty in the house.
18. Are you willing to housebreak a dog? How would you accomplish that?
19. Are you familiar with the use of crates as a training tool for your dog? How do you feel about them?
20. If your new dog does not get along with your other dogs, what will you do?
21. Understanding that a new dog might initially have some problems adjusting, how would you handle the following:
    Accident on rug?
    Leg-lifting to mark new territory?
    Crying at night in crate?
    Jumping on bed or furniture?
    Getting into trash?
    Chewing a table leg or shoe?
22. What behaviors do you absolutely not want to deal with?
23. Will you be willing for us to visit your home with all family members present before the new dog is placed with you?

We all have enough things in our lives that make us feel guilty. If you have tried your best to make the new dog welcome in your home and the situation still doesn't work, you should feel confident about your effort and leave the guilt behind. Some people have the mind set that any dog that comes into their home will stay, no matter what. Let that be their decision. Everyone's situation is as different as the dogs we love; what one person is able to accomplish might be impossible for you.

What really counts is your commitment to help the dogs you welcomed into your home have a better life. If this can't be accomplished at your house, make a commitment to find a home that will help you meet that goal. In this age of the disposable pet, don't be a part of the problem. To drop off a dog at an already overcrowded animal shelter is not an answer. If you feel that the dog is not fit to be placed into a home, face the problem yourself and have the dog euthanized. If all of us who love dogs take responsibility for the dogs that are a part of our lives, we can make a difference.

SUGGESTED READING

Benjamin, Carol Lea. *Second Hand Dog-How to Turn Yours Into a First-Rate Pet.* Howell Book House, Inc., New York, NY. 1989

Ruckert, Dr. Janet. *Are You My Dog? How To Find Your Best Friend.* Ten Speed Press, Berkeley, CA. 1989

Shook, Larry. *The Puppy Report.* Lyons and Burford, New York, NY. 1992

Chapter Three
MANNERS AROUND THE HOUSE

When people talk about manners around the house for multiple dogs, their expectations are as varied as the dogs they own. However, some of the rules are the same for everyone. No one wants their dog to beg at the table or to bark excessively. This chapter can give you some ideas for rules around the house and show you some guidelines for a happy home that have been used by other multiple-dog owners.

This chapter will also help you discover the absolute importance of the dogs in your family looking up to the humans as the leaders. Since this is not a training book, it does not go into great detail on training techniques, but it does offer guidelines to help you select a trainer or behaviorist, and it suggests training and behavior books that will help you succeed with multiple dogs.

IMPORTANCE OF A TRAINED DOG

In the last chapter we built our pack; in this chapter we will learn how to manage that pack. When you own one dog, you can be more tolerant of certain unruly behaviors, for example, jumping on you while you attach a leash to go for a walk. When you add three other dogs jumping all over you, the doors, and the furniture, it won't be long before your patience is shot, or you quit taking the dogs for walks.

Now, let's say the dogs are trained to sit and wait. It only takes a few extra moments to get everyone sitting patiently, so you can snap on the leashes, open the door and start your walk. Okay, who could walk four dogs at the same time and still maintain control? Have you ever seen professional dog walkers managing six to eight dogs? For those of us who aren't professional dog walkers, we could send two dogs to their crates, walk two dogs, then switch. The point is, the task is made much simpler if your dogs are trained.

Private or Group Lessons

What criteria should you use to decide if you need to take your dog to a group lesson or a private lesson? Private lessons are nice because of the flexibility in deciding what you will teach your dog. If your dog is aggressive, you will learn to control him and then be able to take him to a group class. If your dog is shy, private lessons will help build his confidence without the distraction and stress of a group class. Once his confidence and obedience is under control, sign up for a group class and finish the job. Your situation might be like Linda's. Linda knew she needed help. Her puppy, Buster (a Labrador/Golden Retriever mix), was the most active pup she had ever seen. He would run until he dropped. Linda thought once he was neutered he would settle down. The neutering did help, but it was not the total answer. Linda knew that she and Buster both needed some training.

In September, when Buster was 9-months-old, Linda called a trainer who happened to live one mile from her. Much to Linda's dismay she learned he was not having any group lessons until spring. Buster needed to learn some manners right now! The trainer had a board-and-train facility where people leave their dog with him for one month, and he trains the dog. Then the owner gets some lessons to learn what the dog has learned. Linda did not want to leave

Buster there, so the trainer suggested that, since Linda lived so close, she come by with Buster twice a day for 30 minutes each visit and go through the training that way. Along with the two sessions each day at the trainer's, Linda also had 15-minute practice sessions with Buster at home.

The private lessons in this situation worked out great for Linda and Buster. They got the training they needed when they needed it. Once the formal lessons were over, Linda had learned enough to keep on working with Buster on her own at home. Buster is now 7 years old and is a great dog. Linda discovered you learn the most about dogs, in general, when you own a dog that is a challenge.

Group classes have some advantages over private lessons, one of which is cost. Another advantage is peer pressure. When you know you will have to perform with your dog at class the next week, you will be motivated to practice. In a group class you have the distraction of the other dogs and their owners. This distraction will help your dog become accustomed to listening to you when in a crowd. You will also learn in a group class that you are not alone. There are quite a few dogs (and dog owners) that need training.

Behaviorist Saves the Day

In this next story you will meet a family that used both a trainer and a behaviorist. Carol and Ken were not planning on owning three dogs, but before they knew it, it happened. One of their dogs started out as the runt of his litter (a Springer/Setter mix), and no one else wanted him. When Carol was approached about the puppy nobody else wanted, she said "yes" and named him Zachery. Carol and Ken got their next dog because the neighbors were neglecting their dog. Carol asked if she and Ken could have the dog. The neighbors said "yes" and Zhyann, a Shepherd mix, was on the road to recovery. Then Carol and Ken wanted to pick out a puppy and got their third dog, a Golden Retriever whom they named Zeus.

Things went along fine until Zeus reached adolescence; then

he started trying to dominate the other two dogs and his humans. Zac didn't seem to mind, but Zhyann took exception to being pushed around. When the fighting started, Ken and Carol couldn't believe what was going on in their house. When Zeus began trying to take over as head of the household, Carol and Ken knew they had their hands full with their Golden Retriever.

Training Begins - Carol asked their veterinarian for advice. He recommended neutering both the male dogs, which they did. It seemed to help, but it was not the total solution. Carol started taking Zeus to obedience classes at a wonderful training facility that used positive methods. Zeus did well in the classes, and Carol enjoyed the training and the instructors. Over the next two years she took the other two dogs to classes, and Zeus took two more classes. Keeping up with the training for all three dogs was time-consuming, but the results were worth the effort.

Unfortunately, they were still having some problems at home, and the fighting seemed to be escalating. The training had helped them gain some control, but the behavior problems were still present. After one particularly disturbing fight that ended with Ken being bitten while he was trying to break it up, they knew they needed more help than the training was offering. Fortunately, Carol had just read an article in the local newspaper about a behaviorist, so she gave him a call. He came to their house and went immediately to the backyard to be with the dogs. As he interacted with and observed the dogs, he asked Carol a lot of questions about how she and Ken managed the dogs and the environment, and about how the dogs interacted with each other. From this information they developed a *Plan of Action* together.

Behavior Modification in Action - The plan worked very well. The key to its success involved gaining more control of Zeus around food, since most of the fights occurred in the kitchen or around Carol for her attention. The first step was to keep the dogs out of the kitchen. Even crumbs on the floor were enough to start a fight, so not allowing the dogs in the kitchen was a simple solution. The next step was to put the obedience training to work at meal times. In the past, Carol just put down the food bowls, and the dogs would eat. Sometimes the dogs would bully each other for the food, and that's when the fighting would start. The plan involved having the dogs sit and wait for dinner, then wait for a command to go ahead and start eating. The plan worked ,and there have only been a couple of minor scuffles in the last three years.

Carol and Ken learned a lot from all this. They have learned it is not always a good idea to get the puppy that is the rowdiest and comes running out to you first, especially if you have two other dogs. The rowdiest puppy is the one that is probably the most dominant in the litter and may also want to be dominant in his new home. Before you get a puppy, find out about puppy temperament testing, and make the selection with your mind, not your heart. Carol learned about canine body language. She can now tell by the look in her dogs' eyes and their body posturing whether she needs to intervene. Thanks to obedience training and the help of a behaviorist, Carol and Ken now have control of a situation that was out of control.

GUIDELINES FOR PROFESSIONAL HELP

If these scenarios seem familiar, you should consider contacting a trainer or behaviorist. In some communities around the country, you do not have a choice of trainers or behaviorists to help with your dog. You might live where there is no one at all. If this is your situation, other options are phone consultations, books, video tapes, or letter writing. The end of this chapter lists some suggestions.

Trainer vs. Behaviorist

The difference between a trainer and a behaviorist is illustrated in the following example: In command training (by a trainer), if your dog doesn't like other dogs, he can learn to sit and stay when around other dogs. The real problem is ignored, and the fix won't work when you are not present.

A behaviorist will give you ways to teach your dog to tolerate other dogs, solving the problem, not treating the symptoms. The selection of the right trainer or behaviorist for you and your dog is very important, so before you pay any money, make sure you feel comfortable with the person and the techniques and methods he or she is teaching.

The best approach by far to all problems with multiple dogs is prevention. Before a specific behavior gets to the point that you feel the need to call in professional help, nip it in the bud. To do that you will need to combine the techniques of training and teaching the dogs in your home. The difference between training and teaching is:

- Pavlov's dogs were trained; they did something because they were conditioned to do so, not because they had any understanding of what was expected.

- When you teach a dog, you instill in that dog an understanding of what you expect from him; you give him the tools to think for himself and make decisions about his own behavior.

Start training and teaching your puppies and dogs the very first day they come into your home. The old wives' tale of waiting until a puppy is six months old before starting training couldn't be further from the truth. Puppies younger than six months have minds like sponges; they learn so quickly it is fun to teach them. The idea that you can't teach an old dog new tricks is also a myth. As long as a dog can walk, he can be trained. Both you and your dog will enjoy the time together.

If your house has been a little too chaotic and you realize you need some help, the first thing to do is to talk to your local veterinarian, Humane Society, or groomer. These professionals may be able to give you the name of a person or training club that can help. Look in the newspaper or the phone book. Try asking some friends who have dogs that are well-behaved. In most cases, well behaved dogs don't happen without some kind of training. In fact, some friends may also be having problems with their dogs. The solution might be getting together once a week with your dogs and using one of the many training books available as your guide.

Selecting a Trainer

You now have the names of a few trainers in your area. The first contact with that person or organization will probably be on the phone. From that call you will be able to tell a lot about that person, and about his or her training techniques and classes by asking questions such as the following:

- When are classes?
- Where are the classes held?
- How many students will be in the class? (If there are more than eight people in the class, there should be an assistant or second instructor.)
- What is the cost?
- How long have you been training people and their dogs? Do you attend training and behavior seminars and workshops?
- What kind of things will my dog learn?
- What teaching methods will you use? Are the methods positive and motivational?
- Can I come and observe some classes?
- Can the entire family participate in the training?

In some cases a person may be a great dog trainer and have lots of AKC titles on his or her dogs. That does not mean he or she is a good trainer of people. In obedience classes, the instructor does very little actual dog training. The instructor teaches you how to train your dog. The lion's share of the training is done by the student at home, not in the class. An important part of any class is that you be given hand-outs to remind you what was taught in class for your practice sessions at home. The repetition of the obedience exercises you learn in class instills in your dog a certain *stress tolerance*. This stress tolerance the dog learns from dealing with the repetition of obedience work will be evident any time your dog encounters a stressful situation and still obeys.

Selecting a Behaviorist

Behavior problems in the multiple-dog home can be mind-boggling. A good book or two on solving canine behavior problems will give you some ideas of techniques to use and a basic knowledge of canine behavior. Reading up on the subject will give you the information you need to select the right behaviorist to help with the dog problems you may be having. When you live with multiple dogs, ignorance is *not* bliss.

If you need a behaviorist to help with your dog problems, the behaviorist will need a thorough understanding of your dogs and your interaction with the dogs. The behaviorist should make a trip to your house to make an assessment. If you go to the behaviorist with your dogs, you have taken the dog away from the problem area, and the behaviorist will not be able to properly assess the situation. In fact, even the presence of the behaviorist in your home can change the dynamics of the situation. The problem might be handled in one visit, but follow-up visits are generally in order. Be honest about the situation, and don't make excuses for your dog's behavior. With that information in hand, together you will be able to develop a Plan of Action that will work for you and your dog. Make sure you and your family are committed to seeing the plan through to its end. What good is it if you are unable or unwilling to put the plan into action?

YOUR ROLE: TRAINER AND BEHAVIORIST

Multiple-dog ownership takes some planning. You will do most of the training at home. The advantage of training at home is you will be training your dogs around the cause of the behavior problems, for example, a coveted toy. As a result of the practice at home, you will gain control and establish yourself more firmly as the leader of the pack.

It is important to train one dog at a time. This one-on-one time is also critical for developing a strong bond with you and each of your dogs.

Barking When Left Alone

If your dogs bark when they are left alone, the problem could be they are not getting that one-on-one time. If every time you take one dog outside to train, those left in the house bark continuously, you have a problem. Will it ever stop? Here are some suggestions.

*   If you still have only one dog, train it before you get your second dog. Dogs learn from each other, good and bad, so a trained dog in the home is worth two in the crate.
*   If you already have the second dog and now realize your mistake, take them both to class. Since it is you who is actually being trained during the class, find an instructor who will

let the two dogs share the one training class. This will only work if both dogs are at the same level of training.

- If you have two dogs, you might get a third dog to keep the dog left inside company. If that seems too drastic, save a special chew toy to give the dog in the house only when you are outside practicing.
- If you have three or more dogs and are kicking yourself for not starting sooner, you can begin the training by insisting on certain manners around the house, such as sitting for every treat. In-house training is effective if done in a positive manner using lots of praise and treats.

Train your dogs every day. This does not necessarily have to be obedience work only; for example, you can work in some fetch, or play a hide-the-toy game. Owning more than one dog is a commitment of time.

Paws off the Counter

Now that we are on the subject of in-house training, what are some of the things you should expect from "good" dogs around the house? Staying off the kitchen counters is a good place to begin. If your dogs are getting some tasty morsels off your counter every now and then, it could be hard breaking them of that habit. Remember this rule of training: intermittent reinforcement is stronger than consistent reinforcement. If your dogs occasionally find treats on the counter, they will check every time they pass the counter. The best solution is to keep tasty treats off the counter tops in the first place.

That solution might seem too easy, but sometimes the easiest solutions are the best. When living with multiple dogs, you will most likely need to make adjustments. Dogs eat what they find; if you don't want them to eat it, don't leave it where they can find it. Dogs will also chew on things in their territory; don't leave your good shoes lying out on the floor if you don't want them chewed up. Dogs don't understand porcelain; if you don't want it broken, don't put it where dogs might bump it, or knock it over, etc. It's very similar to the way babies explore things; that's why you put covers on your electrical outlets, locks on your cabinets, and the poisons and medicines out of their reach when there's a baby in the house.

However, as far as food on the counter goes, you might need to make sure that the dogs know to stay off. To proof that, set up a situation with food on the counter and dogs in the area. Once you set up the situation, you will be able to make *corrections* because you are in control. A correction is designed to interrupt or stop your dog momentarily from the undesired behavior. A correction will probably not eliminate the behavior or teach the desired behavior. If you make the correction after the food is eaten, that correction is a waste of your energy. The dog has already been rewarded. Keep an eye on the dogs from another room; as soon as you see the nose twitching, say "no." At this point you have made the correction while the dog is thinking about misbehaving. That is the most effective time to make the correction.

Keep watching from a distance. The dog might forget the whole thing and go lie down. Give lots of praise. This is the result we are after. The dog might continue sniffing the air and start formulating a plan. Too bad for him! You have a better plan. If he jumps up on the counter with his front paws, you come flying out of your hiding place using your best growly voice, waving your arms, and generally causing a scene. As soon as the dog has all four paws on the ground, praise him. This is the desired behavior.

If your dog is clever and realizes you won't always be home to reprimand, you might have to set up a situation that will cause a correction without you being there. You can set up a situation with the use of shake cans as the correction, by setting the cans on the very edge of the counter. Shake cans are aluminum cans (e.g., soft drink cans) with a few pennies or small stones in them. When your dog jumps up to get the food, the cans crash to the floor and startle the dog. The dog receives the correction, and you are not even in the room. In order for this to work, the correction must be more alarming than the reward of the food is pleasant. The correction has stopped the action for the time being. Don't forget the most important part of the process is teaching your dog what you want, and that is to stay off the counter. Praise, praise, praise, anytime the dog is in the kitchen and all fours stay on the floor.

Dogs on Your Furniture?

When it comes to furniture, most people agree that the furniture in the house is for humans first, then the dogs. In some homes, the dogs have certain pieces of furniture that are for the dogs only. In other homes, the dogs must decide if the furniture is covered and not go on it when it is not covered. However, in our multiple-dog home, I have to say if my dogs wanted to be on the furniture I'm sure they wouldn't check to see if it was covered. Some homes proclaim "No dogs on the furniture at anytime!" This rule leaves no room for mistakes, is easy for dogs to understand, and has no gray areas.

I used to be a no-dogs-on-the-furniture owner, but as my sofa and love seat have aged, my resolve has softened. Now we welcome and encourage our dogs to share our furniture with us. The standard rule around most multiple-dog homes is the best seat in the house is for the humans, and the dogs should give up that place without an argument. If the dog growls at you for moving him, he has a behavior problem, and you should consider not allowing that dog on the furniture at all until he moves without discussion. Remember, you are the boss, or alpha, and your word and wishes are final.

My Bed or Their Bed?

Many people who responded to the questionnaire allow their dogs to sleep on their beds with them. Dogs in bed with you can be the start of behavior troubles and is one of the first things you should change if you are having any problems with your dogs. Once your dogs start sharing your bed, you have compromised your position as alpha because the dog sees you as an equal now. Sleeping on the bed with humans is a common solution for the puppy blues and getting a handle on housebreaking. So when you start letting the dogs on your bed, be aware you might be starting something that could get out of hand .

The subject of the dog not getting off the bed when asked is bound to come up with certain types of dogs. When you let an alpha-type dog sleep on the bed with you, he then considers himself your equal. He may even start thinking that he is letting *you* sleep in *his* bed. If the dog won't get off your bed without growling, the privilege should be denied. To get the dog off the bed, you might try getting his favorite toy and coaxing him off the bed with that. Once he is off the bed, close the bedroom door, make the bedroom off limits, call a behaviorist, and get control of the problem.

Letting your dogs sleep on the bed with you is a hard habit to break if you later change your mind. Before starting this habit, consider the fact that you may be sleeping with your canine companions for the next fifteen years. In some situations, people have moved to another room because the dogs have crowded them out of their beds. Since I work at home, writing, boarding dogs, teaching obedience classes, and managing our five dogs, I don't want any dogs sleeping on my bed. By the end of the day, I have had my fill of dogs. My daughters, on the other hand, are away from their dogs all day while they are at school, and they do sleep with their dogs.

Crates as Beds–Crates can be put to good use as beds for dogs. Younger and more unreliable dogs are put into their crates with the doors closed at night to sleep. Dogs that are trustworthy can have the doors left open for the night. With the doors of their crates left off or open, your dogs can still do their job of protecting the house from intruders.

This brings up the subject of dogs being locked in crates and not being able to be save themselves in case of fire. One respondent has her dogs' crates right by the door; then if there is a fire, they will be easy to rescue. I had never considered the dangers of dogs in crates and the possibility of fire or other disasters. So when deciding where your dog will sleep locked in a crate, have a rescue and escape plan ready, just in case there is a fire. Better safe than sorry!

Potpourri

Another standard restriction around the house for owners of big dogs is no rough-housing or rowdy playing inside the house. "Take it outside." This is often not true for people who own small dogs; small dogs can get a good portion of their exercise playing indoors. As a rule, the respondents do not allow their big dogs to play indoors, but encourage their small dogs to do so. Sorry big dogs, but I bet you get more walks outside!

Other rules that would be worth the effort to teach your dogs are these:

- Never leave the front door without permission. Variations of that are no going out the door without a leash on, or no going out the front door at all.
- The command "crate" means go to your crate, from anywhere in the house. If you don't use crates, the command "place" will send your dog to his predesignated place.
- Teach the dogs that the word "off" means sitting patiently and waiting to be greeted by company. Some owners like being jumped on when being greeted by their dogs, though most guests who come and visit do not. Teach the "off" command and you have an option.
- Teach your dogs to stop barking on command. Use the words "no bark" or "enough." The verbal command "enough" is especially effective because it emulates the low, slowly escalating growl used by the mother to stop pups from doing something. If the verbal command is not enough to stop the barking, you might want to use a shake can or a spray bottle with water in it. As soon as the dogs stop barking, praise with "Good dog!"

- When you give out treats, have your dog sit and make him earn the treat. This exercise is also very important for maintaining your role of alpha.

HUMANS VS. DOGS FOR LEADERSHIP

The leadership role in a canine pack can belong to either the humans or the most dominant dog in your household. There are some things you can do around the house to establish yourself and all humans as leaders. Here are a few suggestions:

- Be consistent in your expectations. When something is off-limits for your dogs, it should always be off-limits. If it is "no" today, it should be "no" tomorrow. Eliminate the gray areas, and you will eliminate the confusion. But remember to praise for correct behaviors.
- Give the dogs daily body rubs. The rubs not only make your dogs feel loved, they also show the dogs that you must be allowed to touch them anywhere. For example, if you discover that your dog does not like having his feet touched, that is your cue to touch his feet ten times during the day. To change your dog's mind about having his feet handled, have his favorite treats handy, then touch his feet and give a treat. It won't take long before your dog starts to think, "Oh good! She's about to touch my feet!"
- When walking your dogs, practice a few obedience commands, such as sits and recalls, during the course of the walk. Occasionally take your walks in new territories where the dogs will rely more on you for instructions.
- Have short obedience sessions at random times throughout the day, in a variety of places, indoors and out.
- Use obedience training when playing with your dogs; for example, have them sit and wait before your throw the ball. Make sure the dog comes back to you with the ball. If he doesn't, use a long line for a while, so you can guide him back. The dog's reward is that you will throw the ball again.

• When you are doing things around the house and the dogs are in the way, make the dogs move rather than stepping over or working around them.

AGGRESSION ON THE HOMEFRONT

If you are having serious problems involving aggression in your house, let me caution you about breaking up dog fights. Stay calm! When you use screaming and aggression to break up a dog fight, you are a part of the dog fight and a prime candidate to be bitten. Your best bet to avoid serious injury to any of the parties involved is to break the fight up with water, either from a dish that is handy or your garden hose. The use of water will make it possible for you to avoid the situation of one or both dogs having their teeth sunk in and you pulling, causing tearing.

In some situations of fighting amongst pack members, the best recourse is do nothing at all, and let the dogs work it out for themselves. If this is your choice, you will most likely end up with one dog that is dominant and another that will respect that position. I know for myself I would have a difficult time walking away from a fight between two or more of my dogs, or even standing passively by waiting for the outcome.

Respondents gave these suggestions as methods they have used to break up fights. Both involve pulling, so use them only if all else fails. Grabbing the back legs of the aggressor might be enough to get the dog to let go; if not, you can try pulling the dog away. Again, let me caution that if you need to pull, you might be the one to cause any damage. The other suggestion was, if you have a blanket handy, throw that over one of the dog's heads to break up the fight. If you are alone and your dogs start fighting, you might try pulling the dogs as a unit, by both of one dog's back legs, to an open door. Then close the door, separating the dogs. After your heart stops pounding, go to your nearest telephone, and get some help from a behaviorist or trainer.

Some other thoughts on aggression in the multiple-dog home involve negative attention vs. positive attention. When there is a dog fight, the instigator is going to get a lot of attention. Granted, it is not praise, but it is attention. This is similar to children who misbehave to get their parents attention. Keep in mind that negative attention can be equal to positive attention. After you have broken up the fight and are putting the pieces of the puzzle together to figure out what happened, examine your part in it. Have you been treating the dogs according to their pack ranking? Have you been too busy at work or with the kids to do more than pat them on the head for days?

Jean-Marie has had to deal with aggression in her dog pack. She owns four dogs: a terrier mix, a female Labrador, and two of her offspring (a male and a female). All of the dogs are spayed or neutered. When Jean-Marie goes to work, she puts the two offspring into an outdoor kennel where they get along fine. The trouble starts when she gets home and lets them out. They are, of course, very excited, and as a result of the excitement, the male, Polar, aggressively attacks the female, Gretchin. To break up the fighting, Jean-Marie started using the nearby hose (the one she normally used for cleaning the kennel) to spray Polar. This was very effective, and she only needed to do this a few times before he would go into his dog house to escape the spray. Eventually, Jean-

Marie only had to touch the hose, and Polar would go into his dog house. Now Polar knows when Jean-Marie comes to the kennel, he should go to his dog house while Gretchin gets out first for some personal time with Jean-Marie. After Gretchin is in the house, Jean-Marie lets Polar out, and he gets his one-on-one time. The other two dogs, Poppy, a terrier mix, and Gypsy, the mom, aren't involved in the conflict. In fact, Poppy, a spayed female and the smallest, is the alpha dog in this pack.

To be a successful owner of more than one dog, you need patience, a knowledge of dog behavior, proven training techniques, a sense of humor, and a love of dogs. To be a successful dog in a multiple-dog household, the dog needs manners, an ability to live with other dogs, a secure yard, love, and food.

In the next chapter we will look at feeding multiple dogs. Problems and solutions are described along with some helpful suggestions that will make things go smoothly for you and your dog.

SUGGESTED READING

Dog Fancy Magazine
P.O. Box 53264
Boulder, CO 80322-3264
(303) 786-7306

Dog World Magazine
P.O. Box 6500
Chicago, IL 60680
1-800-247-8080

Campbell, William E. *Behavior Problems in Dogs.* American Veterinary Publications, Inc. Santa Barbara, CA. 1985

Palika, Liz. *"Fido, Come!"*. Doral Publishing, Wilsonville, OR. 1993

Pryor, Karen. *Don't Shoot the Dog! The New Art of Teaching and Training*. Bantam Books, New York, NY. 1985

Rogerson, John. *Understanding Your Dog*. Popular Dogs Publishing Co. Ltd., London, England.

Videos worth watching:

Dunbar, Ian. *Socializing and Beginning Obedience*
Dunbar, Ian. *Behavior Problems and Household Etiquette*
Dunbar, Ian. *Sirius Puppy Training Video*

Kilcommons, Brian. *Good Owners Great Dogs,* 1991

To find a the name, address, and phone number of a dog obedience instructor in your area contact:

American Mixed Breed Obedience Registry (AMBOR)
205 First St. S. W.
New Prague, MN 56071

National Association of Dog Obedience Instructors (NADOI)
Peg Prudden
P. O. Box 432
Landing, NJ 07850

Chapter Four
FEEDING A CROWD

The dogs are all anxious. It is time for dinner. What are they going to eat? Is the food that you are serving your dogs nutritionally sound? Should you vary their diets? Are your dogs overweight? Where are they going to eat? The answers to some of these questions can be very confusing unless you are a canine nutritionist. Some of the answers are different for every dog and group of dogs. This chapter will answer those questions and solve some of the problems you might encounter when you feed more than one dog.

DIET

You should not overlook the importance of a healthy diet. It will help your dog live a long life and can cut down considerably on trips to your veterinarian. To decipher the complicated information concerning a healthy diet for your dog, you almost need a degree in dog nutrition. I don't have a degree in dog nutrition, but I am concerned about the diet I feed our five dogs. My veterinarian sells only one brand of dog food, and the smell of that kibble makes me almost gag. It might be a good quality food, but it has to work for me, too. I don't have direct access to experts in the field, but I have read as much on the subject as I was able to find. Some of the articles were like reading Greek. The information I am going to share here will help the average dog owner solve this puzzle.

Dogs are like us in some nutritional aspects; we are both *om-nivores*. An omnivore is an animal that does best when eating both animal and plant materials. This does not mean you should feed your dogs chicken, potatoes, and a salad for dinner. In fact, that would be a very unhealthy meal for your dogs, because dogs' nutritional needs are also different from ours. Here are the basic elements in a balanced diet for dogs:

- Protein is one of the primary elements in a healthy diet. When dogs digest protein, either animal or plant, it is turned into *amino acids.* Amino acids are the elements that break down the protein, so the dog's body can put it to work. Dogs need 22 amino acids to thrive. Ten of these they can't manufacture himself, so they must get them every day from their diet. The rest of the needed amino acids the dog's body can manufacture itself.

- Fats are also an important element in a balanced diet. The more active a dog is the more he needs fat in his diet. Whether from animal's or vegetable's, fats are also important to the absorption of fat soluble vitamins like A, D, and E. Fat is the most efficient form of energy in dog food.

- Carbohydrates are also energy suppliers, but the energy comes from starches and grains, such as corn and rice. Carbohydrates travel through the bloodstream and break down during the digestive process. Carbohydrates are responsible for quick energy.

- Minerals and vitamins are important to the function and tissue of the body. When carefully balanced, they help prevent serious health problems. The vitamin and mineral needs of dogs are easily met in the high-quality commercial dog foods available today.

Quality In—Quality Out

Your dog's stool is a good indicator of your dog's health and reaction to his diet. In a multiple-dog household, stools are a very important factor, for obvious reasons. Most multiple-dog homes pick up stools once a day. There is no better way to monitor your dog's health than cleaning up the dog's bathroom area and watching for worms or diarrhea. If your dog's stools are sloppy, smelly piles of waste, you would do well to examine your dog's diet.

Labeling

Check the ingredients and make sure the food you are feeding is meat-based, not cereal-based. The ingredients listed on the back of the package are listed in the order of weight, for example, beef meal, wheat flour, ground whole wheat, wheat milburn, corn gluten meal, etc. At first glance, it may appear that this food is meat-based because beef is first on the label, but this can be misleading. For example, if the weight of the beef meal is 21 percent, wheat flour is 20 percent, ground whole wheat 19 percent, wheat milburn 15 percent, and corn gluten meal is 12 percent, the food actually has more cereal than meat as the base and may be the reason you are having trouble keeping the dog's area clean or are having trouble housebreaking your dog or puppy. Cereal-based foods tend to cause larger stools, usually because your dogs are not making use of most of what they are eating.

The terminology on dog food labels is pretty straightforward. If the label says meat, beef, chicken, or fish, it means the clean flesh from the slaughtered animals. The term *by-products* indicates the nonrendered clean parts, other than the meat, of the carcasses of slaughtered chicken, beef, fish, or lamb. Beef, chicken, or fish *meal* refers to the rendered tissue and by-products of these animals.

When you look at labels on dog food, you must recognize the difference between dogs and humans and understand the dogs' need for fat in their diet. When I'm shopping, I look for fat-free or the lowest level of fat listed on the label for myself and my family. The opposite is true for your dogs. Dogs need fat in their diet for energy and good health. High fat content in your dogs' food is generally an indicator of high digestibility and palatability. Digestibility is indicated in the stools' size and volume.

Keep in mind while shopping for dog food that although the higher-quality food is more expensive, you will be feeding less of it than the lower-quality food. Your dogs will also digest and put to use more of the ingredients in the high-quality foods, reducing the size of their stool. Dr. Kellee Roberti also notes that the recommended amounts to feed on the dog food packaging tend to be on the high end of how much to feed. Remember each dog is an individual, and this must be taken into consideration when determining the amount that is right for your dogs.

Back to the original question, "What should I feed my dog?" As a general rule, if you are buying the best-quality dog food you can afford and your dogs have healthy skin and coats, you are doing just fine. No dog food is perfect for every dog. You may need to experiment with a variety of commercial dog foods to find the one that fits the needs of your canine family. With the variety of dogs in most multiple-dog families, you might have to feed a few of types of dog food: puppy, senior, high performance, and maintenance. You may also need a couple of different brands to keep all of your dogs healthy.

FEEDING IN ACTION

Let's take a look at how some of the respondents feed their multiple-dog families, keeping in mind good nutrition and affordability.

Balancing Act

This next example is from a family of four Doberman Pinschers and two humans, Deborah and Kevin. Deborah and Kevin had two Dobermans (a black and tan male Damon, and a fawn female Molly). These two dogs had puppies and they kept a blue female Desdamona, because she was so precious. Now Deborah and Kevin were only missing a red Doberman, and they would have one of every color. Deborah put the pressure on her husband, and before Kevin knew it, they had their fourth dog, Cherokee, or "Cherry" for short.

Feeding four big dogs is expensive. They used to feed the dogs one of the high-quality dog foods you can't buy in grocery stores. Even with both working, the cost was prohibitive, so they started buying 50 pounds of a high-protein dog food and mixing it with their regular dog food. They also buy the big cans of less-expensive meat food, watching for sales, of course, to mix with the kibble. For variety, Deborah shops grocery store sales for macaroni and cheese dinners, which the dogs love mixed with their food.

They also love pot pies (bought on sale), which Deborah heats up and mixes with the dogs' dinners.

The dogs are fed twice a day. In the morning around 8:00AM, they get dry food, and in the evening, about 6:30PM, they get dry mixed with canned or table scraps. If the dogs don't get two meals a day (breakfast and a hearty dinner), they lose weight because they are so active. The dogs spend the day outdoors and in the evening come indoors. They eat their meals in the kitchen, except Cherry, who dines alone because she used to fight with the other dogs about food. This multiple-dog family has found a balance between good nutrition and budget.

It's All Yours

Norman and Bonnie's multiple-dog family has small dogs and strives for variety and nutrition. The budget isn't a big issue because there are five Toy Poodles and three Chihuahuas. The dogs are *free fed,* that is, the dry food is available at all time. Each evening between 5:00PM and 6:00PM, each dog receives a dish of special food. This consists of one tablespoon of cottage cheese, four green beans, two nuggets of canned food, and one sliced grape. For added variety, when strawberries are in season, the dogs get a half of a strawberry instead of the grape. The dogs love it!

VARIETY CAN BE THE SPICE OF LIFE

In both of these multiple-dog families, the owners went to some effort to provide nutrition and variety to their dogs' meals. While researching this chapter, I read two conflicting opinions on variety in canine diets. One opinion is that dogs do not require variety in their diet. If you have a food that your dogs like, stick with it; they won't get tired of it. That opinion was from a representative of one of the major dog food companies. The other opinion is just the opposite and comes from a veterinarian. His belief is that variety in a dog's diet is good for the dog, both physically and emotionally. Keep in mind that any table scraps that you add to your dogs diet should be no greater that 10 percent of the total ration. If you keep nutrition for your dogs in the forefront of your thought, you will be able to find a happy medium between health, nutrition, and variety.

WHEN TO FEED

Let's answer the question about how often you should feed your dog each day. This again seems to be something that is a matter of opinion. Some people think adult dogs do fine being fed once a day, others say twice a day, while still others keep a dish of food available at all times. Most of the multiple-dog families I heard from feed their dogs twice a day, although there were some good reasons for feeding once a day or free-feeding. I will share the situations and reasons with you, and you can decide which is best for you and your dogs.

Free-Feeding

Let's look at free-feeding. This will only work if all of your dogs are willing to share, are not overeaters, and all of your dogs are eating the same type of food. Obesity and dog fights are the big drawbacks with this method of feeding multiple dogs—not to mention some dogs will eat less, or only occasionally, and even may be chased away from the food by other dogs in the family. It is also difficult to determine whether any of your dogs are "off their feed" for a few days.

If you always have a dish of dry food available, you will be less likely to worry if you are detained in traffic. It also would work well for people who have a hard time sticking to a set schedule. The dogs seem to regulate themselves with some preferring to eat in the morning, others in the afternoon or evening. If you have dogs that don't share but don't fight, you can set out two food dishes and keep them filled. If you have a dog that is overprotective of the food bowl and free-feeding is the method you choose, a good approach is described best by Cathy.

Cathy has four female dogs: one Yorkshire Terrier (Bebop), and three Papillons (Emily, Katie, and Sophie). The food is left down all the time, but it seems they only eat when Cathy is at home. Her problem was Bebop. She was guarding the food, so Cathy put down two bowls of food. This did not seem to solve the problem, so she tried putting down fifteen bowls of food for Bebop. Since Bebop could not guard all of the dishes, she now just guards the bowl she is eating from and the other dogs can enjoy their food.

Time can be the determining factor for free-feeding. Michelle found that separate feeding times for her two Dobermans, Blitz and Mitzie, was too time-consuming, and the dogs seemed to lose weight on that schedule. She decided to try free-feeding and started by putting small amounts out for them. This has worked out great for them because now the dogs eat as they burn calories.

Free-feeding can also be the source of other problems in the multiple-dog home. One of the main problems is *obesity*. Obesity is a condition characterized by excessive bodily fat. An obese dog looks thick. You should be able to easily feel the shape of the ribs or lower back. In an obese dog, the ribs and back will be covered with a layer of fat. Once your dog is obese, it becomes harder to control its weight. Dogs are not very good at regulating their calorie intake; a dog may eat because one of the other dogs is eating, not because he is hungry. Dogs may also eat out of boredom.

To control obesity, you need to regulate your dogs' food intake and increase activities. Often, you must also change your attitude toward your dogs. Don't equate your love of your dog by allowing him to overindulge. You are not doing your dog any favors by letting him go through his life overweight. The health risks associated with obesity can reduce the dog's longevity and his ability to function.

Another problem with free-feeding can be housebreaking. If your dog has access to food any time of the day and you are at

work, will he be able to relieve himself in the appropriate location? With a regular feeding schedule, you can regulate your dogs'
elimination habits.

FEEDING ON A SCHEDULE

When you feed your dogs on a regular schedule, for example,
twice a day, that gives your dogs two very exciting times to look
forward to each day. Most dogs have very little excitement in their
lives, and meal time is certainly one of them. Why not thrill them
twice a day instead of once?

The most important reason for feeding your dogs twice a day
is a medical reason. That reason is *bloat*, especially if you own
large, deep-chested dogs, such as Great Danes, German Shepherds,.
Labrador Retrievers, and Boxers. Bloat is an abnormal accumula-
tion of gas within the stomach that causes the stomach to distend
or even rotate. This condition becomes even more serious if the
stomach twists or rotates (*torsion*). This condition happens very
quickly and can lead to death if not treated immediately. Some of
the symptoms of bloat to watch for include signs of abdominal
discomfort, such as whining, pacing, getting up and lying down,
stretching, looking at the abdomen, anxiety, and unproductive attempts to vomit.

Although not proven, you might reduce the chances of bloat
in large, deep-chested dogs by following these suggestions:

- Limit water intake immediately after meals.
- Feed two or three times a day instead of once.
- Be sure someone is home to observe your dog after he eats.
- Limit vigorous exercise for at least an hour after meals.

If you feel your dog is at risk for bloat, or has already survived bloat, you should discuss bloat management with your veterinarian.

LOCATION, LOCATION, LOCATION

Where should you feed your dogs? If your dogs can all eat side-by-side without conflict, this is probably not an issue. But if you have one dog that eats slowly, one that eats fast, and another that wants all the food, you have a problem. Here are some suggestions you can try; you should be able to find one that works for you.

- Feed the dogs in separate rooms. Each dog will learn which room is his and will probably go there and wait for room service.
- If you use crates, you can feed the dogs in them. If you don't have enough crates for all of your dogs, feed the fast eaters in crates. Then they won't be able to wander around and bother the slower eaters.
- Feed the dogs one at a time, with the dog that is not being fed waiting with you.
- Use a different corner for each dog, and be sure to always feed the same dog in the same corner.
- Stand and monitor the dogs during meal time.
- Teach the dogs to sit and wait for their dinners and not to start eating until their name is said along with an "okay."
- Feed the slowest eaters first and the faster eaters last.

Char and Tom have come up with some great solutions for the mealtime problems they were having with their four dogs. Gwendolyn is a Lab cross approximately 13 years old. Char received Gwen as an anniversary gift 12 years ago from her husband (he's a veterinarian). Gwen was allowed to run free by her previous owners and was shot as a result of her roaming. Her injuries cause her to be urine and stool incontinent. Sadie is a 13-year-old Dachshund/Sheltie, rescued as a 6-month-old puppy after being hit by a car. H.T. is a 17-year-old Cocker Spaniel cross that belongs to Char's dad and has been staying with them for the last two years. Last but not least, the youngster in the family is a 2-year-old

Pembroke Welsh Corgi, Buster, described as "delightful."

With the various ages and health problems among the dogs, it takes ten minutes to prepare the twice-a-day meals. This can be a challenge with the four dogs weaving through Char's feet. The excitement of meal preparation keeps the "olds" young. Since the dogs are hungry at mealtimes, they don't dawdle over their food. The regular schedule also makes it possible to regulate Gwen's bathroom habits and avoids accidents in the house. The main problem is fast and slow eaters. Buster is the speed eater, and when he finishes, he tries to wander over and "share" with the other dogs. The other dogs are not interested in sharing, so Char stands watch during mealtime like a police officer at a busy intersection. The movements of the other dogs during mealtime bothered Buster, so Char cut out one side of a cardboard box (it has a bottom, three sides, and no top). Char puts Buster's dish in the box so he can't see the other dogs while he is eating. Mealtimes are now stress-free at this house.

The health advantages of feeding your dogs in separate areas at scheduled times should not be overlooked. You will be able to monitor your dogs' food intake and make sure each dog maintains its ideal weight. You will also be able to feed your dogs special diets if needed and not worry about the wrong dog getting the wrong food. You will avoid fights and each dog will be able to enjoy his food without being harassed by the dogs that eat faster.

WATER, NECTAR OF THE GODS

In addition to feeding your dogs, don't forget to leave fresh, clean water available for your dogs at all times. If you live in an area where the water has a bad odor or offensive taste, you may find it necessary to use a water purifier. Also keep in mind that dogs that eat canned food consume less water than dogs that eat mostly dry food.

A good way to keep water from being splashed when the dogs are drinking in the house is to keep the dogs' water bowl in a low, flat container like a kitty litter pan. If you have three or more dogs, you may want to keep the water outside in buckets, so the dogs will always have water available. Remember: fresh water everyday, watch your dogs' water intake right after meals as this might be one of the causes of bloat.

SNACKS

Your dogs are now well-fed, the stress has been removed from mealtime, and they are getting fresh water daily, but what about treats? Follow the same guidelines you use for selecting your dogs' food: read the labels. Be careful to look for artificial colors and added sweeteners in dog treats. These ingredients might include: corn syrup, molasses, sucrose, or dextrose. Be aware that artificial colors have been linked to some behavior problem.

We all know that treats should not be a major part of your dogs' diet, just like goodies shouldn't be the main staple in our diets. But we all like treats, and I'm sure we all will feed our dogs treats from time to time. Don't forget that treats can be a significant source of calories for your dogs, especially if several members of your family are giving treats. Kellee Roberti, D.V.M. suggests breaking the treats into small pieces. After all, it is not the size of the treat that makes your dogs happy, it is getting it from someone they love.

You might be interested in making your own snacks for your dogs. Making dog treats to sell at a bake sale for your local humane society or shelter can be a good fund-raiser. Here are a couple of recipes that your dogs are sure to enjoy.

Healthy Dog Treats

Pureed beef liver
Garlic powder
Whole wheat flour
Bran flakes
Wheat germ
Rolled oats
Eggs

For each pound of liver, add one tablespoon garlic powder, two eggs and enough of the other dry ingredients to reach the consistency of cookie dough. Use a lipped cookie sheet and spray with

a vegetable oil spray. Spread dough ½-inch thick and bake at
350° F for approximately 20 minutes for soft cookies or leave in
the oven until the dough is as crisp as you wish. Refrigerate for a
short time or freeze.

Cheese Cookies

2 cups all purpose flour
1¼ cups shredded cheddar cheese
2 cloves garlic, finely chopped
4-5 tablespoons water
½ cup vegetable oil

Preheat oven to 400° F—bake a four-inch bone pattern out of
cardboard or use a cookie cutter of your choice. Combine flour,
cheese, garlic, and oil in a food processor. Cover, whirl until mixture is the consistency of course meal. With the machine running,
slowly add water until the mixture forms a ball. Divide dough into
12 pieces. Roll out each piece to ½-inch thickness and cut into
bones. Do not re-roll scraps. Bake on ungreased cookie sheet for
10 to 15 minutes or until bottom of cookies are lightly browned.
Cool on a wire rack, and refrigerate in an air-tight container.

Canine Bones

1 pound beef liver
2 large eggs, shells washed
1 cup low-fat cottage cheese
1½ cups wheat germ
Approx. 3¼ cups whole wheat flour

Boil liver until no longer pink in the center (about five minutes). Save the liquid in a one-cup measure. Add water to make
one cup if you come up short.

Put the liver in a food processor. Break in eggs, including
shells. Puree and then add reserved liquid as needed to keep mix

ture moving. Scrape sides often. Scrape mixture into a bowl; add remaining liquid, cottage cheese, wheat germ, and three cups of flour. On a well-floured counter or plastic cutting board (wood may pick up the liver odor), knead dough until it is no longer sticky. Add flour as needed.

Shape dough into ball. Clean counter. Add fresh flour. Dust ball with flour, then roll to ½-inch thickness. Cut with bone-shaped cookie cutter or shape by hand. Set cookies slightly apart on greased baking sheets. Bake in 300° F oven until bones feel firm (about an hour). Transfer to racks to cool. Store in air-tight container in refrigerator or freezer.

Now that we are all feeding our dogs properly, the next step is housebreaking. Chapter 5 gives you a brief overview of standard housebreaking and paper-training procedures. Then we will troubleshoot a variety of the problems that you might encounter as a multiple-dog owner.

SUGGESTED READING

Boyd-Smith. *No Barking At The Table Cookbook*. Lip Smackers. 1991

Brennan, D.V.M., Mary L. *The Natural Dog*. PLUME, New York, NY. 1994

Pitcairn, D.V. M., Richard M. *Dr. Pitcairn's Guide To Natural Health For Dogs and Cats*. Rodale Press, 1982

Volhard, Wendy. *Back to Basics*. Top Dog Training School. 1984, (315) 593-6115

Chapter Five
HOUSEBREAKING SOLUTIONS

You were sure your dog Duffy, a Miniature Schnauzer, was housebroken. She had not gone to the bathroom in the house since she first came to live with you three years ago. But you have recently added another dog, Vicki, to your happy home. Vicki, a Long Coat Chihuahua, came from a kennel, had never been housebroken, and was four years old. Does this story sound familiar to you? It does to me; it is my home and my family's dogs.

When you live with dogs of all ages and sizes, you can bet you will have some housebreaking accidents. In this chapter, I will share with you some housebreaking problems, solutions, and cleaning suggestions. I have also included an outline for housebreaking that makes it easy for most dogs to catch on to the idea of "doing their duty" in a designated area. You can't talk about housebreaking without including clean-up ideas, so I'll include the most popular ideas that respondents shared. You can decide which ones will work best for you.

PERSONALLY SPEAKING

Back to my "happy" home: This all started two years ago when we brought Vicki home. Almost immediately, Duffy started having accidents in the house. I had housebroken many dogs so I wasn't really concerned at first. I thought I could take care of this in a few weeks—no big deal. I was about to learn more about house-breaking than any one person should have to know.

Crate Time

We had four dogs at the time; they had free run in the house and we had no problems. So I thought I would just go back to the beginning and put Vicki and Duffy in crates, take them outside regularly, and praise them when they "did their duty." If they elimi-nated outside, they would earn some free time in the house. I watched them carefully during their free time but I was still find-ing potty spots and "presents" tucked away in hidden places. I wasn't able to watch carefully enough. As a result, I added more crate time and more careful watching. This went on for almost a year. When it seemed like we had it made, it started again. The housebreaking never was 100% reliable. Also during this time, my older dog, Annie, started taking a steroid that was causing her to drink more water and urinate more often. She hadn't had an accident in the house in 14 years; now she was having them quite often. Good grief! I was taking steps backward instead of forward! The dogs were spending so much time in their crates now, it didn't seem right, but they were ruining our home. That was not right either.

Damage Control

The bathroom areas of choice were the dining room (with the oriental rug) and one of the extra bedrooms upstairs. When I cleaned those carpets, then they picked the office area and one of the kids' bedrooms. The rubber-backed throw rugs were fair game, too. Annie would just go wherever she was when she needed to go. We did not want to divide up our living area with gates, but it seemed inevitable. My husband, John, built and installed some custom gates. All the dogs were now confined to the kitchen and family room. The pressure was off the rest of the house, but the problem was not over.

Inspector Carol

Duffy and Vicki are my daughters' dogs, and the girls sometimes forget and give the dogs free run of the entire house. When this happened, found the "accidents" again. Neither dog left very big spots so I usually did not find them right away. More than once when I caught them in the act, I hurried them immediately outside to finish. I was even showing them the accidents (*not* rubbing their faces in it), verbally correcting them ("Bad dog!"), then taking them outside and using the cue words "Hurry up." I was on housebreaking Plan N, and we had started with Plan A. We were making headway, but we were still not close to the finish line. It was very frustrating.

Renewal of Vows

The topic of housebreaking was common dinner table conversation (only in a multiple-dog family could you talk about the elimination habits of your dogs over dinner and not have your meal ruined). One more time we made a pact to watch the small dogs more carefully, crate them when we couldn't watch them, go outside with them, praise like crazy when they went outdoors, and be more diligent about letting them out on a regular schedule.

Now I let Annie out every hour to relieve herself, which she does very quickly, rain or shine. Duffy in particular does not like to relieve herself outside if it is raining. Since we live in the Pacific Northwest, it can get quite tedious standing outside in the rain saying "Hurry up!" over and over. The gates are up, there are now crates always set up in the family room and the office. Both daughters have crates in their rooms.

A Day in the Life of...

Here is the schedule that we basically try to follow: All dogs go out first thing in the morning, then I feed Vicki and Duffy breakfast in their crates. The other dogs eat on the deck, weather permitting. After my daughters leave for school, I take Vicki, Duffy and the rest of the dogs outside with me while I clean up the dog yard. I then spend some time in the kitchen cleaning up after the morning rush and the dogs have some free time. Before I head for my office (it used to be our living room) I put Vicki and Duffy in their crate. They like to share one big one. The big dogs go in the dog yard or, if it is raining, they come into the office with me. Annie stays free in the gated area and sleeps.

Mid-morning I let Annie out quick and get another cup of coffee. Later, I take an hour lunch break; during that time I slam a sandwich and take the dogs on walks. Then it is back to the crate for you-know-who and back to work for me. Before you know it, the kids are home from school and they let their dogs out of the crates and take them outside. By then I'm out of the office, in and out of the car, and finally in the kitchen making dinner. The dogs get fed and we eat dinner. Whew! Time to relax!

The moral of this story is you might go years with dogs that all housebreak like a dream, but if you bring in one dog that is a problem, what are you going to do? Some folks at this point have the problem dogs become outdoor dogs. I don't think a Chihuahua and a Miniature Schnauzer were made to be outdoor dogs. Chapter 6 describes the lives of some happy outdoor dogs; this might be the solution for your problem dog. In our family, I have tried my best to deal with the accidents and still save the investment my husband and I have made in our house. We are almost there. Hopefully, we will soon have an accident-free house.

MEDICAL CONDITIONS

Before we go any further with housebreaking information, you should be aware of the fact that a housebroken dog that suddenly starts having accidents might have a medical problem. The sudden inability to control the bowels may be a symptom of something more serious. At this point, a trip to the veterinarian may be in order to put your mind at ease and get on with the training.

Older spayed females have a tendency to become *incontinent*. They are unable to control their urine, due to a deficiency in the hormone estrogen. This can easily be treated with medication prescribed by your veterinarian. Young and old dogs of both sexes can become incontinent and it can also include loss of bowel control. Other causes of incontinence can be kidney stones or other ailments of the kidneys, bladder infection (cystitis), or diabetes. This is by no means meant to be a complete list of medical reasons for incontinence, just a reminder that a trip to your veterinarian should be the first step to consider.

HOUSEBREAKING ABCs

Many people use the following basic housebreaking guidelines. It starts with *confining* your new dog or puppy as soon as you bring it into your home. Confining in this context can be any one or combination of the following:

- Keeping the dog on leash.
- Putting the dog in a crate (airline or wire).
- Using a playpen.
- Closing off a small area or room with a baby gate.

You should plan on letting your dogs outside on a *regular schedule*. The schedule should include the following times:

- As soon as the dogs wake up in the morning and after naps.
- After eating.
- After periods of play.
- Before bed.
- Every hour to start with, increasing the time depending on the dog's age.

The Great Outdoors

When the dogs go outside to eliminate, always be sure you accompany them so you can say the word(s) that will teach them to relieve themselves on command, for example, "hurry up," "go potty," "go on," and "outside." The words can be anything you want as long as you use the same ones each time. Another good idea is to clap your hands rather than say a cue word(s). Keep in mind you will be using this cue in public, so a hand clap may be less embarrassing then saying "go potty." Go outside with your dogs so you can be right there to give verbal praise and maybe even a food treat for a job well done.

Ring Them Bells

To encourage your dogs to ask to go out, give praise at the door, then proceed outdoors. Another idea is to have bells or chimes hanging from the door. Then teach the dogs to ring the bell to let you know if they need to go out. To start with everytime you let the dog out, *you* ring the bell. Only ring the bell when you are letting the dog out to eliminate and not when you are letting him out to play. I suggest you teach the dog to ring the bells with his nose and not his paws. We taught our Newfoundland puppy, Belle, to ring a bell with her paw. We had been trying to teach Duffy and Vicki to ring a bell to go out and they just looked at us like we were crazy. Belle caught on very quickly and would ring the bell fifty times during the course of a day. We were all trained to respond quickly to sound of the bells, because we never knew if she wanted the bathroom or just to get a breath of fresh air. It drove us crazy and that big paw of hers ruined our door. Our mistake may have been rewarding for both ringing the bell and going to the bathroom. A respondent who has used the bell method makes the point that once the dog can ring the bell, he only gets the reward when he rings the bell *and* has gone to the bathroom. There is no reward for just ringing the bell and going outside.

Paper Training

Ideally, you should try to train your dogs to go outside and skip the use of papers all together. Sometimes that is not possible, so here are some ideas about paper-training:

If you use newspapers, you have to contend with the newsprint that is on them, or rather, the newsprint that ends up on the dogs. When the newsprint gets wet, it gets on the paws and can get tracked all over. Some folks use a layer of paper towels on top of the newspaper to cut down on the newsprint mess. This works really well with small dogs, but large dogs often drag the paper towels off of the newspaper, especially if the dog steps in the mess; the light paper towel sticks to his feet and drags the mess all over the floor.

If your confined area is in a carpeted room, first put down a sheet of plastic like a large plastic garbage bag, followed by layers of newspaper and then the paper toweling. If you have a large sheet of linoleum available you might want to protect your carpet with that and then the layers.

If your dogs are small or very young, you might want to use a low pan like a kitty-litter pan, lined with paper towels. If your dog is larger, you might consider using a crate tray lined with newspaper. These trays are available at pet supply stores or you can order them through a pet supply catalog.

Another good suggestion is to use the pads you put under a baby when changing diapers. They are absorbent on top and waterproof on the bottom, which is ideal. In this day and age of reuse and recycle, they are also machine washable. This will be my next step here at home if our house soiling problems continue.

CRATES: HAVEN OR PRISON?

Let's talk a little bit about the use of crates for confinement and the proper and improper use of them. Most dog people agree that crates are a great training tool if used properly. This means confinement of no more than four or five hours at a time when you use a crate for housebreaking. When you are away at work for eight to ten hours at a time, you should leave the dog in a confined area with papers in one of the corners of that area for elimination.

Long-term crating (expecting your dog to not relieve himself for eight to ten hours at a time) is not fair to the dog. Have you ever been in the car with someone who would not stop for you when you had to go to the bathroom? It can get very uncomfortable. I don't want my dogs to ever have to feel that way because of me.

If you need to confine your dog in a crate for long periods, try to make arrangements for someone to come over midway through the day to take the dog out for relief and a leg stretch. If it is impossible to make those arrangements, confine your dog in an area that can have an elimination area in it. Since the use of crates can be controversial, here is a list of some of the advantages and disadvantages of crates:

Advantages

Dogs can be kept in crates in the area of the house where the family spends the most time.

Crates offer security for the dogs. The dogs can relax and sleep without having to be constantly on guard.

In case of a natural disaster, crates offer safety for your dogs.

Can offer a safe haven for dogs that suffer from separation anxiety or destructive tendencies.

A young or problem dog that is kept in a crate when unsupervised will stay in his home rather than being brought to a shelter.

A crate keeps your dogs safe when riding in cars or trucks.

Disadvantages

Crates take up a lot of precious space in a small house or apartment.

It is easy to abuse the use of crates by stashing a problem dog in it rather than taking the time to train.

The humans might have to deal with some guilt feeling about caging their dogs.

When you own multiple dogs, it can be expensive to have a crate for each dog.

Some dogs cannot tolerate the use of crates, and may actually have seizures when put in such a confining area.

Keeping puppies or dogs confined for too long of a period of time and the puppy being forced to use his den as a bathroom.

FINE TUNING

Now let's say you get home from work, you take your dogs directly outside and, Hallelujah! They take care of business. If one doesn't go, you can pop him in his crate without guilt because he hasn't been in it all day. Then you can try again a little later. Or, if he has been in his crate all day, you can keep him with you by keeping him on his leash while in the house.

Dogs are pack-oriented, and you can put that to work for you when it comes to housebreaking. If your new dog is a puppy, it will probably want to be like one of the big guys and follow them outside and copy them. If your new dog is an adult, peer pressure may motivate him to follow the rest outdoors and do his business outside.

Is There a Carpenter in the House?

A dog door installed in your home can also help eliminate housebreaking problems. You won't have to keep an eye on the door all the time to be ready to let the dogs in and out. The dogs can come and go at will, which gives the dogs freedom they would not have without a dog door. If you live in an area where you don't feel safe with an open dog door while you are gone, you can keep the dogs confined in the house while you are away and open the dog door only when you are home. This will also work if you worry about dognapping and don't want the dogs outside when you are not home or can't supervise them.

If you live where you don't have to worry as much about the criminal element, a dog door can be a relief if you don't always get home on a regular schedule. Then you don't have to worry about the dogs waiting around with their legs crossed, anxious for you to get home and let them out.

Your new dog will get the hang of the dog door very quickly with the other dogs in your pack using it. A dog door and peer pressure can really speed up the training process in this situation. I sometimes think a dog door could be the answer to our problems, but neither Vicki nor Duffy like stepping outside in bad weather. I'm afraid we would go to the trouble of installing a door and still have the problem. Another drawback of a dog door is dogs with muddy feet coming and going as they please.

"..., this Land is My Land..."

What if your problem is scent marking? This problem is generally thought of as a male dog problem. Let me assure you, female dogs can get into scent marking too, especially if they are the dominant sort. To get a handle on the scent marking problem, first consider having your dog spayed or neutered. You can also start outdoors by not letting the dogs mark the entire neighborhood when you take them on walks. When you go on your walk, give the dogs a chance to relieve themselves before starting (remember to use your cue words), then start walking and correct any other attempts to urinate and mark. When you get back home, give the dogs another chance to go. This has two benefits:

- You eliminate the dogs' feeling of ownership over the entire neighborhood.
- It keeps your dogs' waste in your yard. With all of the anti-dog sentiment and anti-dog legislation going on today, keeping your dogs' waste in your property can go a long way toward increasing tolerance for and acceptance of dog owners, especially those with multiple dogs.

If the scent marking problem is chronic and you just can't stop the dog from marking in your house, you can always try putting pants on that dog. This solution will only work if your dog is the right size and has the right build. Little boys' training pants or diapers with a slit added for the dog's tail both work well for this problem.

WHAT GOES IN MUST COME OUT

Remember, when your dogs defecate while out on a walk, it is your responsibility to clean it up. Place a plastic sandwich bag over your hand to grab the bulk, then turn the bag inside out over the stool. This works great. I live in a rural area and carry a hand shovel with me when I walk our dogs. I can just fling it in the woods and out of the way. Cleaning up after our dogs is the best way to assure our continued use of parks, trails and beaches.

Since we are on the subject of our dogs' waste, let's talk a little bit about cleaning up the dogs' yard. To keep track of your dogs' health, you need to examine their stools everyday. You can check for diarrhea, worms or blood in the stool. Also for the health of your dogs, you should clean their exercise area everyday. The most common method for disposal is simply putting the waste in a bag, in the regular garbage. But with more and more landfills refusing to accept "yard waste," which includes animal feces. Here are some suggestions for what to do if your garbage hauling company won't accept animal feces:

*   Burying it in a pit dug for that purpose.
*   Purchasing a small septic system made especially for pet waste.
*   Use a home-made septic system made from a plastic trash can with holes in it, buried in a pit of sand.

This next suggestion came from Kathryn who used to own three Shelties and one Irish Setter. (Two of her dogs recently passed away due to complications of old age.) She picks up stools as they are deposited and puts them into a small, lined trash can she empties every other day into the regular trash. This method works out especially well in the winter months. In the summer, you will have to empty the trash bag everyday to avoid excessive odor. But having the small can available outside at all times has made it possible to keep the dog yard nice and clean.

Our dog yard is covered with gravel. The main reason was to help keep the muddy paws under control, but it also makes the clean-up easy. The smell of the urine can get quite powerful if the weather and wind conditions are just right, so we spray our dog yard twice a month, one time with an odor neutralizer, Nilodor® and the other with a germicide, Outright™'s Ken-Care™.

ACCIDENTS WILL HAPPEN

If you own multiple dogs or are about to own multiple dogs, you will become an expert on cleaning up accidents. My dogs range in age from puppy to 15 years. I clean up urine and vomit with some regularity, stools less often. My carpet has very few stains as I can usually come up with something to remove a stubborn stain. I must admit, though, that I am looking forward to the day when I can have the carpet removed from our family room and have it tiled. Then I plan on having rubber backed, machine washable, area rugs where they are needed.

The toughest spot I have encountered was when one of our dogs got a nasty cut on his pad. I think he stepped on a sharp piece of ice out on the deck. It happened while I was busy with a 4-H meeting and I didn't notice it right away. By the time I did notice, there was blood everywhere. My husband started the clean-up using a enzyme cleaner, but pretty soon the spot was getting bigger and bigger. Luckily, I had already started getting questionnaires and quite a few dog owners were very happy with the results they got with Resolve® Carpet Cleaner.

I wasn't able to get to the store until the next day, so I covered the spots with wet towels to keep them from drying and used the Resolve® the next day. The blood came out miraculously.

I haven't tried all of the following methods (yet), but enough people mentioned the same thing that I have to believe that these are good ideas and encourage you to try them if your spots are tough.

The best way to start is to catch the dog in the process so you can bring him outside right away and start to clean the accident up before it dries or soaks in. Soak up as much of the urine as possible with paper towels or old towels. Don't step on the paper towel to speed up the soaking action. If you step on the paper towel, the urine gets on the bottom of your shoe, then you track it around the house. A dog's sense of smell is much better than our own, so you have now spread the urine smell everywhere you have walked.

The most popular solution was water mixed with white vinegar. This was either mixed half and half, or 2/3 water and 1/3 white vinegar. Try both and see which is best for you. The white vinegar solution works best on accidents that are fresh. Put the vinegar solution on the area after you have soaked up as much of the urine as possible. Then soak up as much of the vinegar as you can.

Resolve® Carpet Cleaner was the next most popular cleaner. This comes in two forms at most grocery stores. One is a spray foam in an aerosol can and the other is a spray in a refillable bottle. Both work great. The directions for proper use are on the can or bottle.

The next most popular cleaner was the enzyme action cleaner, Nature's Miracle®. This cleaner has worked wonderfully for me for years. It does the job on stubborn, set-in stains and also removes the odor. I have always used this brand of enzyme action cleaner because that is what the pet supply store I go to carries. Any cleaner that has enzyme action will probably work the same.

Another popular cleaning method involves the use of club soda. This method was best described by Mary Ann. She owns three dogs, two Newfoundlands, Cheyenne and Dakota, and a Labrador, Copper. She soaks up the urine with a clean white towel (or two), then saturates the spot with club soda. She lets that sit on the spot for a minute or two, then soaks that up. The final step is pouring on cold water and letting that sit for a minute or so, then soaking that up. She says she never has a stain.

Murphy's Oil Soap® was also suggested as great cleaner for all types of fabric. I use it on my wood floors and it works well for that. Sandy has four German Shepherds, Wolf, Bella, and Guinan. On carpet accidents, she first uses an absorbent powder, like Booda® 911, that you sprinkle on and vacuum up. If necessary, use a diluted solution of Murphy's Oil Soap®. Take a rag or scrub brush and scrub. Sandy says not to pour the Murphy's directly on the fabric; make it is diluted with water. On strong odors, she uses white vinegar followed by the Murphy's Oil Soap®. Next time I have a tough stain or odor, I'm going to give the a try.

Another interesting suggestion for stains on carpets is to soak up as much urine as you can get, then saturate the area with a diluted solution of Listerine® . That should keep the dogs from returning to that area again.

Uncarpeted are easier to clean. Hardwood floors will need

more care in the selection of cleaner, Murphy's Oil Soap® might be a good choice, but check with a wood floor expert in your area. You can use a disinfectant, bleach, or any all-purpose cleaner on linoleum or vinyl floors. Make sure you check the ingredients on the bottle; you should *not* use an ammonia-based product to clean up a urine accident. The ammonia in the product will only accentuate the ammonia in the urine and if the stain wasn't urine in the first place, you might be adding a urine scent where there was none before.

All cleaners have an odor of their own, so it is your tolerance of that odor that will determine whether the product is suitable for you. On stubborn stains with a strong urine odor, you might need to clean the area several times over a few days. When you need to work on a stain over the course of a few days, keep the area moist with wet towels to prevent it from drying. Once the area is dry, the stain tends to set in.

Owning a steam cleaner for rugs can help keep things clean and sweet-smelling. Better yet would be having a carpet cleaning service come clean your carpets on a regular schedule. This seems like the easiest solution, but it is also the most expensive, too. Michael and Olanka have six dogs; Boo, a Belgian Shepherd, Kiki, a Bulldog, Lance, a Labrador mix, two Pit Bulls, Coco and Diamond, and a fostered Boxer named Augie. (All of the dogs are spayed or neutered.) Olanka's suggestion for cleaning up housebreaking accidents is to have someone else do the cleaning. That's the best suggestion I read!

Problems encountered with housebreaking can be some of the most frustrating. By using some or all of the suggestions in this chapter you should be able to devise solutions to the problems your dogs are having. Your solution might be having your dog start living outdoors. Chapter 6 describes what is involved when a dog calls the great outdoors home.

SUGGESTED READING

Delmar, Diane. *The Guilt-Free Dog Owner's Guide.* Storey Communications, Inc., Pownal, VT. 1990

Heloise., *All New Hints From Heloise A Houshold Guide for the 90's.* Perigee Books. New York, NY. 1989

Kalstone, Shirlee. *How To Housebreak Your Dog in 7 Days.* Bantam Books, Inc. New York, NY. 1985

Chapter Six
OUTDOOR DOGS

There are many reasons why dogs live outdoors. Some dogs actually prefer the great outdoors to living inside the house. My Newfoundland, Belle, gets too hot in the house and prefers to be outside (although she is welcome inside anytime she wants). Another reason dogs are kept outdoors is because the dogs' owners are renters, and their landlords will not allow dogs in the house. Other reasons might include allergies, unwillingness to live with dog hair, inability to housebreak some dogs, or dissention among pack members.

In this chapter, I will describe how owners of outdoor dogs have kept those dogs a part of the family, even though they live outside. Each area of the country has special needs; for example, some areas are cold and others hot. We will look at each area of the country where you might find a situation that is like your own.

Not only is the climate different all over the country, but so is the habitat. People with multiple dogs live in rural and urban areas. The needs of the dogs in each of these situations are also variable.

Y'ALL COME BACK NOW, YA HEAR?

The first thing I want to talk about in reference to outdoor dogs is confinement. In Chapter 5, we talked about confinement used for housebreaking. When talking about confinement for outdoor dogs, the criteria is a little different. A fenced yard is essential. Some respondents lived in very rural areas on 20 or more acres, and some of these folks don't fence their dogs. This works for them because their dogs stay at home and don't roam. However, not all dogs stay close to home, and the hazards to free-roaming dogs are many: being shot or poisoned, being hit by cars, getting lost, chasing wildlife and farm animals, or killing wildlife and farm animals.

Fence 'em

Here is an example of a man who lives on 80 acres in Oklahoma and has had to start confining some of his dogs because of their refusal to stay home. This is how he has it worked out.

Vladimir lives with five dogs: two Airedales, two West Siberian Laikas, and one Karelian Bear Dog. He also has 60 free-ranging chickens. Vladimir was able to train all of his dogs except the female West Siberian Laika to leave the chickens alone. As a result, this dog cannot be allowed to be free until the chickens are roosting. She wasn't too fond of that situation, so she was becoming a barker.

Another problem was the two Airedales who liked to go off on their own hunting expeditions. Although Vladimir's 80 acres are adjacent to a public recreation area and the dogs stayed within these limits for the most part, it was not a situation that he was comfortable with, and he considered it a problem. He also worked out an arrangement with his neighbors. They all became familiar with each other's dogs and agreed not to shoot the dogs if they came visiting. The plan was to send the dogs back to their own home and to make a phone call if the problem continued.

Vladimir solved his problems by building a 40 x 120 ft pen and placing five dog houses inside. The fenced area has shade trees in it and is partly on the prairie. The pen also has double gates to prevent accidental escapes. The two West Siberian Laikas are kept in the fenced area except when being supervised or exercised. The Karelian Bear Dog is kept in the pen or allowed to be free during the day because she is the most reliable of his dogs.

During the day, the Airedale bitch is either chained or in a smaller pen by the chicken's barn. At night she is allowed free because she is the best watch dog. The male Airedale is free during the day but at night is chained by the chicken coop. If both Airedales are free at the same time, they are off to hunt, which they never do if they are not together. The main job of these dogs is to keep predators away from the chickens. They chase away coyotes and sometimes tree a bobcat. Vladimir enjoys the wildlife and never shoots at it, but he wants to make sure it respects his dogs and his chickens.

The dogs in the pen can play and dig holes to their hearts' content. Vladimir takes care of them in their pen at least three times everyday. In addition, he takes three of the dogs (never all of the dogs together) almost every evening for at least an hour walk in the woods and prairie, or down to the lake. The dogs can run, play, and generally act like dogs. If for some reason Vladimir cannot take the dogs on the walk, he just goes to the pen to spend time with the dogs and feeds them something special.

The barking problem is under control, and there is never barking during the day anymore. If any of the dogs bark at night, the Airedale bitch will investigate the reason and take care of the problem. Although Vladimir's dogs live outdoors, they are very much a part of his life. He has worked out his problems and now keeps his dogs out of harms' way through confinement.

Chain 'em

Keeping dogs out of trouble can take some juggling until you have the money to build the necessary fences. Susan from Ohio owns seven dogs and lives on a few acres. Most of the dogs came to her out of the woods or were dropped off on a nearby highway. Five of her dogs live in the house, and two of them are outdoor dogs.

Since Susan has moved from the city, her finances are more limited and her two outdoor dogs were kept on 40-foot chains by their dog house for awhile. This was not ideal, but it was better than risking their lives on the nearby highway. The dogs now have a 50 x 60 ft fenced area with two igloo-type dog houses in it. The dogs are also exercised, one at a time, in the 200 acres of woods behind her house.

Keeping dogs chained to a dog house does not mean leaving the dogs chained for days on end without ever letting them off of the chain. A dog kept on a chain without social interaction with its owners could become aggressive, stir crazy, a chronic barker and/or unmanageable. A dog's life was not meant to be spent staked to a dog house without interaction with his family. But if you spend time grooming, exercising, and socializing your dogs, it can be done without harm to your dogs' psyche.

Kennel 'em

A perfect example of the good life for outdoor dogs is this family from Montana. Linda has ten Siberian Huskies and two mixed-breed dogs. The dogs are all spayed and neutered except one of the female Huskies. Since this family camps both summer and winter, Linda feels the dogs need to be comfortable with outdoor temperatures. Another reason the dogs live outdoors is because Linda likes a hair-free home. Since she isn't spending any of her free time cleaning the dog hair in the house, she has more time to spend outdoors with the dogs.

The dogs come in the house for special attention and for medical reasons. All of the dogs are housebroken, socialized, and obedience trained. When the dogs are in the house, they know they should lie down when told. They also know they are not allowed on the furniture unless they are invited.

In the winter, the dogs are kept outside, chained to dog houses with dry straw as bedding. The dog houses are the plastic igloo-type for ease in cleaning. In the summer, the dogs are kenneled in a building with a cement floor and wire on the sides and front. Each kennel is cool and holds two dogs for companionship, plus they have plywood beds to lay on. The kennel is near Linda's cabin so she can see and talk to the dogs through the windows, and they in turn can watch her throughout the day.

Linda spends a minimum of four to six hours a day caring for and exercising her dogs. These dogs are allowed to do the job they were bred for because Linda exercises them all at the same time by running them as a team pulling a sled in the winter. In the summer, Linda and her family hike and backpack, and the dogs are always included. In fact, on their summer vacation to Waterton National Park in Canada and Glacier National Park in the USA, they took all the dogs with them. The dogs seemed to enjoy being a real part of the family and took well to vacationing. Linda also stresses that you must be responsible when traveling with your dogs and leave the area you were in cleaner than when you got there.

The three families described here all live in rural areas; now let's look at outdoor dogs that live in urban areas. City dogs can live just as happily outdoors as country dogs. They can also be a part of the family even though they don't live indoors.

Condominium Living

Catherine owns two dogs: Baby Bear, a Cocker/Springer mix, and Max, a Doberman. Both dogs live outside in a large backyard. Their house is an enclosed patio, and then they have a "condo" within the enclosed patio. The condo is 4-feet high by 4-feet wide by 4-feet deep; it is elevated off the concrete, has wall-to-wall carpeting, and maid service (Catherine).

Because the dogs are outside dogs, they don't have many restrictions. They are not supposed to bother the plants on the patio, although occasionally there is a casualty. This family loves their dogs, or "babies," as Catherine refers to them. Just because dogs live outdoors doesn't mean the family doesn't love them.

On a sad note, shortly after this was written, Catherine wrote to let me know that her precious Baby Bear has to be put to sleep at 13 years old due to pneumonia and kidney failure. On a happier note, they have added Squirt, a spaniel mix, to their family. In true spaniel tradition, she took over their lives and hearts.

Club Med

The next family lives in Texas and has six dogs of varying ages, shapes, and sizes (they are spayed or neutered). Pam makes sure their dogs have it all; they have a swimming pool that is four-feet deep with concrete blocks for steps. When Pam and her husband are doing yard maintenance, such as cutting the grass or spraying the yard, they have a special kennel that the dogs go into to stay out of harm's way. This kennel is also used for newcomers or dogs that should be kept quiet.

The dogs do not live in the house, although two of the dogs come in at night to sleep. The house has a 56-foot covered patio across the back of the house, and each dog has an igloo type dog house. In addition to that, the dogs have a 14 x 6 ft concrete block dog house, or bunk house. During stormy weather the dogs like to bunk in there together. The bunk house used to be made out of wood, but one of the dogs ate part of it. The wood didn't settle too well, and it took a trip to the veterinarian and $385 to get her back on track.

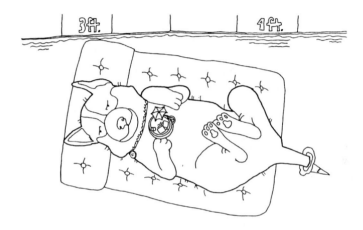

Yards Galore

Tresa has five dogs (all spayed and neutered). Her two Rottweilers, two Scottish terriers, and Airedale live with her in Oregon. Her 13-year-old Scottie, McGregger, lives in the house and is let out on a regular schedule. The 5-year-old Scottie, Charolett, goes to work with Tresa at her grooming shop and also lives in the house. The 10-year-old Rottweiler, Ritz, and the 3-year-old Airedale, Hattie, are either with Tresa during the day, in the kennel, or in one of the fenced yards. These two dogs also sleep in the house. Last, but not least, is her 5-year-old Rott, Dieter. He is an outdoor dog and has the job of watchdog.

There are three separate yards and two kennels for the dogs. Two of the yards are on either side of Tresa's home, and the kennels are also next to the house. Both of the yards open with gates into a big 2/3-acre yard fenced with economical field fencing. The dogs are not allowed to run in the big yard unless Tresa is at home.

Hattie, the Airedale, is an escape artist and cannot be out at all unless Tresa is with her, as she can go over, under, or through any barrier. When no one is home, Dieter is put in the fenced area that includes the front door of the house. The older Rott is put in the other small yard or one of the kennels.

Tresa has the dogs' insulated houses in the kennel areas. The houses are wood and were the houses her Dad had used for his Labradors 30 years ago. They have required some maintenance over the years but still get the job done. The kennels are 1/2 six-foot solid cedar fencing that help block the wind and offer shade, and 1/2 chain link. In front of each kennel is a tree that shades the kennel in the summer; when the leaves fall in the winter, the sun warms the kennel area.

Obedience training has been Tresa's hobby since 1971. All of her dogs are obedience trained, housebroken, and crate trained. They are very much a part of her life. The main reason Dieter is an outdoor dog is simply because he prefers to be outside.

Once again it is clear that when you are dealing with multiple dogs living in all parts of the country, each situation is different. As I read the responses to the questionnaires, it was clear that the dogs that lived outdoors could be just as happy as those that lived in the house with their owners, because these outdoor dogs are still a part of their owners' lives. They are not just left out in the back-yard. These outdoor dogs have proper shelter for the climate they live in and are exercised, groomed, trained, and socialized.

FENCING

One of the biggest investments for the outdoor dog is fencing. Fencing can be either chain link, wood, or underground electric. The type of fencing you decide on will depend on your budget and your dogs. Your best bet for making the right decision is to talk to others with multiple dogs and find out what has worked for them. Chain link is great if it is installed close enough to the ground or a concrete curb is poured around the bottom. If your dogs do not get along with the neighbors, a solid wood fence will be a big help.

When we were building the fence for our dog yard, we drove around and looked for fences that we thought would contain our dogs, looked nice, and were affordable. After we had decided on a design (we went with a wooden fence), the next step was to go to a few local lumberyards to check on prices. Then we took bids from a couple of builders about installing the fence. We could have installed the fence ourselves and saved money. Since we both work and it was winter when we moved into our house, it would have taken us at least three or four weekends before we could have finished the project.

If you rent your home or relocate regularly, you might decide that underground electric fencing is just the thing for your dogs. The dog wears a radio-controlled device on his collar and will first hear an audible sound when he is approaching the boundary. If the dog keeps going, he will receive an electric shock to keep him in the area of confinement. The advantage of this for someone who rents is that this fence is portable and can go with you when you move. If your dog is a fence jumper, this type of fencing might be the answer for you.

There are also disadvantages to underground electric fencing. This type of fencing does not keep stray dogs off of your property. It is also possible that your dog will endure a shock to get out of the yard but probably will not endure the shock to get back in. With this product you should take a look at your dog and see if it will work for him. Remember, when you are making an investment in a fence—be a good consumer, and do your homework before you build or install your fence.

A DOG'S HOME IS HIS CASTLE

Your next investment for your outdoor dog will be an adequate dog house. You must decide between wood and plastic, choose the features you need, then decide whether you want to build or buy. Some of the standard features any dog house should have are these: enough room for your dog to stand up, turn around, sit, and lie down; the roof should be pitched for drainage, lift off or open for easy cleaning, and have an overhang to keep the weather out, insulation is essential in both hot and cold climates for the comfort of your dogs; the door of the dog house should be either off-center so the dog will have one side of the house that is completely out of the elements, or it should have the option of a hanging door to block drafts, rain, and snow.

Whether the house is wood or plastic, it should be placed up off the ground. This can be done by placing a brick under each corner, or by placing the house on a pallet. In the summer, the space under the house will increase ventilation and help to keep your four-footed friends cool. In the winter, you should consider enclosing the space between the ground and the bottom of the house to keep the cold air out.

When picking the location of the dog house, try to place the door so it faces away from the wind. In the summer, the house should be in the shade and, in the winter, the sun. The color of the dog house is also important, and depends on the climate in which you live. In hot climates, a light color will keep the house cooler. A dark-colored dog house in a cold climate will keep the house warmer for your dog. If you live where the climate has four distinct seasons, consider using a medium color, like khaki.

Bedding for the house is also a consideration. This will depend on your dog. If your dog is a chewer or a shredder, you will probably need to use straw. The downside of using straw is it can harbor bugs, and if your dog has long fur, it can be messy. It can also mix with any mud the dog tracks in to become rock-hard; remember, the Indians made adobe bricks from mud mixed with straw! You may find you will need to chisel it out to clean the dog house. The straw will need to be changed regularly; however, this won't be a problem if you have a garden and you can compost the straw.

Another choice is bean-bag beds filled with cedar chips. The covers of these beds are usually washable, and the cedar chips can also be composted. Old sleeping bags, comforters, and wool blankets (wool is warm when wet) can also do the trick to keep the dogs cozy.

Some dogs prefer to sleep with others in their pack. If this is the case with your dogs, be sure the house is big enough for them. This is the situation at my house. Our dogs have always slept in the house, but since we have gotten Belle (it is too warm in the house for her), we've had to adjust our sleeping plan. She needed to sleep in the garage to keep cool, but she was lonely. Consequently, we were all losing sleep. To keep her quiet through the night, we had Gentry start sleeping out in the garage with her. As the weather got cooler, I fixed up the giant crate by getting it off the ground, draping it with an old sleeping bag, putting old comforters on the inside, and a blanket over the door. Both dogs sleep in the one crate, so I never worry about them being cold.

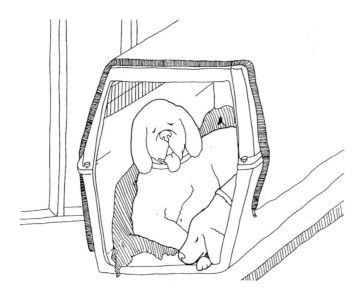

DIETARY NEEDS OF OUTDOOR DOGS

If your dogs are expected to sleep outside, they need extra fat and calories in their diet. One Purina® Pet Care study shows dogs that live outdoors need up to 40 percent more calories in the winter than in the summer. You can add calories to their diets by adding canned food or healthy table scraps starting in the fall. Indoor dogs actually need less food in the winter because they generally are less active. So when you increase the calories in the diet of your outdoor dogs, don't do the same for your inside dogs. When summer comes around again, remember to cut back your outdoor dogs' diet, so they can stay lean and healthy year round.

Dogs that live in the great outdoors actually need more attention than dogs that live in the house. Indoor dogs are with you all of the time, available for pats and friendly words. If you are too busy to give them individual attention, they are generally underfoot and get attention when you ask them to move or when you trip over them. Outdoor dogs need you to step outside. If it is pouring rain, snowing, or hot and humid, you may decide to stay inside.

In Chapter 7, "Dealing With the Guilt," we will look at activities you can do with your dog that will help you to deal with the guilt of not having enough time in the day to dedicate to your multiple dogs. These include outdoor activities, dog sports, therapy work, training, and more.

Chapter Seven
DEALING WITH THE GUILT

If you are a multiple-dog owner, you will at some point feel that

- All the dogs want your undivided attention—at the same time.
- You don't have enough hands to pet them all at once.
- With work outside the home, commuting, and child care, there is very little energy left at the end of the day for the dogs.
- There is not enough quality time with each dog.
- When together as a pack, the dogs are less responsive to human commands than when they are alone.
- It is a problem to train more than one dog at a time.

This chapter gives you some suggestions of things that other multiple-dog owners do with their dogs for recreation. The suggestions will start with ideas that take the least amount of effort and build from there.

This chapter is for me. I have this "guilt thing" down pat. I have always wanted to take our Golden Retriever, Gentry, to get his Companion Dog title (CD). But I'll tell you, with kids, work, volunteer work, and everything else, there isn't time to do it. I always feel guilty. The CD title is earned by getting scores of 170 out of a possible 200 points at three AKC-sanctioned obedience trials, under three different judges. In each exercise the dog must receive more than half of the allotted points. The exercises a dog need to perform at an obedience trial to receive a CD title are

- Heel on leash and perform a figure eight while heeling on leash.
- Stand, without moving, for examination by the judge.
- Perform the same exercises as the heel on leash, but this time off leash.
- Stay where he is left, respond promptly when called, sit straight in front of handler, and return to the heel position.
- Placed in a sitting position, remain in that position for one minute.
- Placed in a down position, remain in that position for three minutes.

Gentry did get his Canine Good Citizenship (CGC) certificate. This test is also sponsored by the AKC and is for both purebred and mixed-breed dogs. The CGC is more casual than for the CD; the training is practically nothing if your dog is well behaved and properly socialized. Some of the things you and your dog will need to perform to get the CGC title are

- Allow a stranger to approach and shake hands with the handler.
- Sit politely and let a stranger pet and examine him.
- Walk nicely on a leash and walk through a crowd of people.
- Demonstrate he has had some training by responding to the "sit" and "down" commands.
- Show confidence around distractions and behave politely around other dogs.
- Last but not least. Maintain his good manners when left with the evaluator by the owner for a few minutes.

The day Gentry and I earned the CGC was a really fun day that we ended by going out for burgers.

All the humans in our family try to make some special time with their dogs. The dogs take turns going with us in the car. When I teach obedience classes, I rotate dogs so they each have a turn helping me. Since our dogs don't have free run of the house, we can bring them with us individually when we are going to spend time in the office. My daughters take their dogs with them up to their rooms while they do homework or listen to music. Read on and I think you will find your guilt going out the window, and you'll soon be enjoying your dogs more.

SUCCESSFUL ENCOUNTERS

Lack of time with each dog seems to be the biggest concern of most multiple-dog owners, so let's look at how two multiple-dog families deal with this concern. An interesting fact about these two families is that their answer to the question, "What would you say is the main problem with more than one dog?" was not "Not enough time with each dog." Both families do manage to spend individual time with each dog. Their answers to this question were:

• None, actually it is easier (with multiple dogs) because they

learn from each other and they play together.
• (Couch space!) Actually, when I want to sleep in, one dog will get worked up to play and wake me and that gets all of the rest of the dogs going. Settling all of them down is a challenge without going outside to play.

Mixing Them Up

Grace owns three dogs: Princess Ski, a spayed German Shepherd, Rudolph, a neutered Anatolian Shepherd; and Samantha, a Lab/Doberman mix, also spayed. These dogs have a very nice life, it seems. Each dog is walked individually at least three times a week. During their walk, each dog receives some obedience training according to how he/she is progressing. Princess is the only dog that has been formally trained, but the others have learned from her. Grace uses the book *How to Be Your Dog's Best Friend*, by the Monks of New Skete, as her guide for training. Other times, they go all together for an off-leash romp in the woods.

The dogs live in the house and sleep on mats in the bedroom. They are not allowed to play roughly in the house, but there is a large bucket of toys from which they can choose their favorites. When Grace goes out, the dogs are either left in the house or tied to their dog houses. The dogs also go in the car when possible, all together or individually. So without taking a lot of extra time out of Grace's schedule, the dogs get plenty of exercise and variety, individually and as a group.

Show Your Dogs

Debbie and her husband, Dan, own five dogs: three St. Bernards, an Old English Sheepdog, and a Lab mix. They go to dog shows with the three St. Bernards, which gets them away from home. That leaves the other two dogs at home for some special time with a good friend of the family that stays with them.

The dogs have free run of the house and the yard through the use of a dog door. The yard is large, and a couple of times a day,

Debbie or her husband goes out to the yard and throws the frisbee or ball for the dogs. Then at least three times a week, every dog goes on a walk with Debbie by itself. The dogs are also trained in obedience, agility, and draft work. This gets the dogs away from home and thinking.

HELPFUL HINTS

You will build a stronger relationship with each of your dogs if you make the time each week to spend time with them individually. This can be as simple as taking one dog with you in the car when running errands. Or you can try a more time-intensive activity such as taking obedience or agility classes and spending time training each dog.

Dogs that live in multiple-dog homes are lucky because they have each other for company and don't have to rely totally on their humans for company. Here are some suggestions for activities with your dog that can fit into even the busiest schedule. These suggestions don't take a lot of training time, and the time you spend training will be a part of the activity.

- Socialize your dogs. Get your dogs used to *every*thing; help them adapt to society. This means walking your dogs in areas where they will encounter horses, sheep, trucks, traffic, sirens, or balloons. This doesn't have to be a big deal. Just helping your dog get used to things that he doesn't encounter very often will help your dog enjoy life. Remember to use praise, encouragement, and treats to help your dog conquer any fears he might have about unfamiliar surroundings.
- Invite a couple of canine friends over for your dogs to play with. This is the easiest way to amuse your dogs. You just need to be sure that the dogs all get along and enjoy the same level of play. Your dogs will sleep well after the canine company has gone home, and if you played your cards right, you did some of your domestic chores while your dogs were busy.

- Quite a few folks enjoy taking the dogs on hikes with them. This requires no real training, only that you and your dogs are in reasonably good shape before you start. It is also becoming necessary to keep your dogs on leash while they are hiking with you, as humans, dogs, and horses are ruining many hiking trails. Use your good sense when hiking; keep an eye on your dogs' paws, especially if the dogs are not used to the rigors of the outdoors. And always clean up after your dogs and yourself.

- Teach your dog to carry a pack, then while you are hiking, he can carry his own water and treats.
- When playing games with your dogs, you should stay in control of the games. Often you will read admonitions to not play tug-of-war with your dog. Actually, plenty of folks enjoy that activity with their dogs by staying in control of the game themselves. To stay in control of a game of tug-of-war, while playing, stop the action every minute or so and have the dog sit or lie down. Then start again. If your dog won't

stop, the game ends and you put the tug toy away for another day. This principle works for all games you play with your dogs. The humans should always be in control.

- Groom your dogs regularly. All dogs need grooming, so why not make it one of those special times you spend together? I like to do it in the evening after the house has quieted down. I'll spread a blanket on the floor and have the dog lie on his side, and I go to work. Brushing, combing, and trimming nails are all a part of this time together. Of course, I spend the entire time telling that dog how special and handsome he is.

Surf's Up

Now bath time is a little different story. I think bath time was best described by Patricia and her descriptions of bathing her five dogs. Her canine family consists of Wembley, a Cocker/Beagle mix; Chelsea, a Springer/Cocker mix; Madison, a Rough-Coated Collie; Ariel, a Golden Retriever/Lab mix; and newcomer Giselle, a Bloodhound. She does the grooming herself for the most part, but she does need the help of two men and a strong boy when it is Madison's turn. (Only kidding, but their help would be welcomed.) Actually, her husband, Vince, gives the needed help with the Collie.

The phrase "tubby time" strikes fear into the hearts of her dogs, so they play hide-and-seek, with the dogs hiding and Patricia seeking. Once that is taken care of, the dogs are bathed according to pecking order. The one exception is Madison, who is saved for last; otherwise, the people would be too exhausted to continue. Madison hates bath time but loves to swim—go figure.

The bathing is done in the basement in the winter and out-doors in the summer. In the winter, the heavy duty pool (actually a sheep dip container) is moved to the basement. A hose runs from the sink to the pool, and another hose is run from the built-in drain near the bottom of the pool to a floor drain.

I don't know of any way to make bath time more fun for your dogs, but if you have someone to help you and you remember to praise and laugh, it might not be so bad for either of you. A nice treat for the dog after the bath can also help relieve some of the anxiety. Oh, what the heck! Get a nice treat for yourself, too!

BUSY DOGS ARE HAPPY DOGS

If you have a little more free time, you might want to get involved in some activities that will take some training time. Here is a sampling of some of those ideas.

Scenting Games

Teach your dogs scenting games. This can start by putting a treat in one of your hands and telling your dog "Find." Once he finds which hand the treat is in, he gets the treat. You are going to be encouraging your dog to sniff. You want the dog to make the connection between the command "Find" and the sniffing action. Once the dog is reliable sniffing your hands and deciding which one has the treat, have a friend put it in his or her hands. Now your dog has to find which hand out of four has the treat in it.

Once this is accomplished and the dog gets better at finding, you can have the dog start finding people instead of treats. One person in the family stays with the dog, and the other goes and hides. At first, the person that is hiding is going to have to give the dog a clue by making a sound. As the dog gets better at finding the missing person, make it more difficult. Remember to always let the dog be successful.

This is more of an individual exercise, so the dogs will have to participate one at a time. This can be accomplished by having the other dogs wait their turns outdoors or in their crates. Or (you know what's coming next) have the dogs wait their turn while they do a down-stay.

If your dogs have been successful with the hide-and-seek games around the house, you might decide that one or more of your dogs would be great at search and rescue work. Search and rescue work can be done by any dog that is good at air scenting and has a handler that enjoys the outdoors.

Agility Activities

Make a playground, or do agility work with your dogs. The playground can consist of tetherball, tunnels, or a stack of logs for climbing. Build their dog houses on stilts, with a ramp for access. For summer, have a pool in which the dogs can cool off.

An actual agility match consists of dogs running up A-frames, going through tunnels, and jumping hurdles in a race with the clock, trying to safely and quickly conquer each obstacle. Many training clubs offer agility training and have agility obstacle courses. Even if you and your dogs don't go into competition, agility work is a great way to build your dogs' confidence.

Flyball

If your dog is a nut about tennis balls, you can teach him to play flyball. Flyball as a sport is a relay race with two teams. Each team has four dogs. One at a time, a dog from each team jumps over four low hurdles, steps on the pedal of the flyball box, which throws a tennis ball in the air. The dog then catches the ball, turns around, jumps back over the four hurdles, and runs across the finish line and back to his owner. The next dog on that team starts off and does his part. The team that has all four dogs come back first wins that heat.

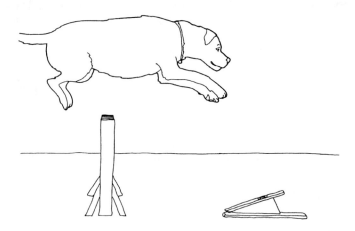

To have your dogs compete at this level, you will need to do quite a bit of training. Your dogs will need basic obedience training since the work is done off-leash. They will also need to be sent over jumps and come back, learn to use the flyball box, and bring the ball back to you.

If all that seems like a lot of work to you, remember, your dogs can have fun with a flyball box right in your back yard. You just need to teach your dogs to step on the pedal that will send the ball flying. Your part in this will be to keep resetting the trigger. Some boxes allow the ball to be launched at different angles. Your dogs will have to keep a sharp eye to see where it is going. The most attentive dog usually gets the ball.

Biking for You, Jogging for Spot

Teach your dog to jog along with you while you ride your bike. This is how Char (we first met her and her canine family in Chapter 4) exercises her active Pembroke Welsh Corgi, Buster. It was easy to teach once Buster was leash trained and had learned the heel command.

This type of repetitive exercise should not be started until your dog is at least a year old. Any younger than that can cause damage to young bones and joints, so check with your veterinarian before you start this activity. With your dog on leash, start with the bike going at a pace just slightly faster than the dog walks. Go in a straight line and command "Heel." It won't take long before your dog will enjoy this time together. As your dog gets better, make the turning around point a little farther and work up to a mile or two at a good clip. You'll get a good workout to boot.

Jogging for Both

How many dogs you jog with at once depends on the dogs' style of jogging. Just like people, not all dogs jog at the same pace. If you have one that really moves along and one that is a lagger, your jog together will be a test of patience. If you want to jog three miles and your dog only wants to go one, are you willing to be flexible?

Remember, any physical activity that you do with your dog may require some extra consideration on your part, depending on the weather. In the summer, you will need to supply water. This can be done with a bicycle water bottle to carry the water and a plastic sandwich bag that serves as a handy bowl. Watch for over-heating; it is usually best to do your jogging in the morning before it gets too hot.

In the winter, ice will probably be a bigger problem for you than for your dogs as far as slipping and sliding. But ice can prove to be painful for your dogs if their paws get cut. You really need to watch for that. Also. be aware of the salt and other things that are put on the roads. These things can cause real problems for your dogs' feet. Clean off all four paws after you jog.

Carting

Teaching your dog to pull a cart is an activity well worth the effort. Your dog will then be able to help you with chores around the yard, and as a result, you will be spending time together. Two dogs can work together pulling a cart, but they should be relatively the same size. Most importantly, before you begin carting, you should make sure your dog is in good health. You should also make sure your dog is well socialized and not easily startled. You will need a properly fitting harness and a cart for this activity.

After your dog has learned to pull a cart, you might want to give demonstrations at local daycare centers. I live in a small community, and when we have a parade, it is a big deal. We are looking forward to having Belle pull a cart in a parade with our little dogs as passengers. It seems like a good opportunity to advertise my dog training business, too.

Skijoring

If your dog loves the snow and running, and if you enjoy being outdoors in the winter and skiing, this might be the sport for you. Skijoring involves one to three dogs pulling a person who is wearing cross country skis. This sport has the potential for lots of fun, but again, you and your dog must be physically capable of the work involved. Also, the dogs must be trained and socialized. This sport requires harnesses designed for pulling and lines for the dogs. You will need a skijoring harness for yourself, skis (Telemark-type work best), poles, and a spirit of adventure.

Dog Sledding

This sport involves a team of dogs pulling a sled. This can be done as a recreational activity or as a racing event. As a recreational sport, you can do it whenever you have the free time, The weather doesn't necessarily have to cooperate. You can always use a wheeled sled for pulling when there is no snow. As a competitive racing sport, dog sledding is expensive and will easily fill up your weekends. The advantage of competition is the camaraderie with other mushers and the opportunity to share information.

Therapy Dogs

Getting involved in a therapy program at a local hospital, nursing home, or other institution will be beneficial for the patients, for you, and for your dogs. Donna and five of her six dogs (Pepper is 15 and Sunny is 7 years old, both are mixed breed; Shady is 9, McGee is 7 and Gracie is 1 year old; these three dogs are all Norwegian Elkhounds) got involved in therapy work after Shady had her CD, Canadian CD, and AKC CDX (Companion Dog Excelent), and she had been tempermant tested by ATTS (American Tempermant Test Society. Donna felt Shady had more to give, so she had her tested and registered as a therapy dog. Ironically, Donna was Shady's first patient when Donna became seriously ill with a debilitating neurological disorder.

When Donna had recovered from the initial attack and diagnosis, she and Shady started visiting a local nursing home. Shady and Donna enjoyed it so much that they slowly started involving more of her dogs and her husband, Ed. Now they visit two homes regularly, and others as requested. Donna, Ed, and the dogs are members of Therapy Dog, Inc. and the Greater Cincinnati Council for Pets Helping People.

This type of work requires your dogs be well behaved, socialized, and absolutely reliable under any circumstances, such as unexpected screaming, hair-, ear-, and tail-pulling, getting tails or feet rolled over with a wheelchair, or getting hit with a cane. The dogs' job is to interact with the patients and brighten their day. It might also include assisting in physical therapy; stroke patients can regain some manual dexterity by petting and feeding the dog. Some patients who have been totally nonresponsive have been known to start talking after pet visits. The dogs can also help rebuild self-esteem. When a 100-pound, 90-year-old woman who can't get her family to visit or her nurse to help her when she needs it sees a 150-pound Newfie obey her command to sit, it causes a complete transformation. Don't shortchange the importance of this job. It's not just fun; sometimes it can be life-saving—literally.

The residents quickly develop favorites and demand to see them each time. Occasionally, a dog we have "assigned" to one home will make a special guest appearance at the other home when the residents request it. Gracie is the most popular guest, because the residents have known her since her first visit at 10 weeks old. They always want to see the "baby," even though she is an adult now.

Therapy dogs must be screened by trained testers. The average pet cannot work well in therapy situations. They get hit, kicked, rolled over by wheelchairs, have food offered and jerked away, hair, ears, and tails pulled, etc. Dogs must be absolutely reliable under all circumstances before exposing them to residents/patients. Using unscreened dogs in therapy can have tragic results for the dogs and the humans. Insurance is an absolute must. In addition to the damage an angry dog, a scared dog, or even a happy, friendly dog can do, if a patient reaches for a dog and falls out of his or her wheelchair, you can be sued for it.

It is also possible that not all of your dogs will enjoy this type of interaction with strangers. But for the dogs that do enjoy it, you will both enjoy the time together and find it extremely rewarding.

Field Trials

Field trials are tests of or a man or woman and his or her dog working as a team. Field trials are meant to test the ability of a breed to continue to perform the function for which it was bred to perform. There are four types of field trials:

1. Hounds are tested on their ability to pursue, either in packs or in pairs, cottontail rabbits or hares.
2. Pointing breeds are expected to assist the hunter in the field. Once the dog scents the game bird, the dog is expected to stop and point. Once the dog is pointing, the hunter can walk past the dog and flush the bird.
3. Retrievers are tested on their ability to fetch and retrieve all game shot by the hunter, from both land and water.
4. Spaniels are tested on their ability to search for feathered game within gunshot range of the hunter. Once the game is located, it is flushed by the hunter into the air. If the bird is shot, the dog should retrieve it on command.

Terrier Trials - A terrier trial is a performance test to see if your terrier's basic instinct is still intact. The test includes entering tunnels, barking, and even some digging. This could be called terrier heaven!

Herding Instinct Tests - These are designed to determine if your herding dog can round up and move a group of ducks, geese, sheep, or cattle.

Lure Coursing - Designed for the sighthound, this tests the natural instinct of these very swift dogs to chase an artificial lure.

Wow! What a list! And that is really only the beginning. The activities you can participate in with your dogs are as many and varied as the dogs we love. To find out more about any of the things briefly described here, look at the end of this chapter for a book or address that can give you more information.

Most importantly, enjoy your dogs, include your dogs in as many activities as you can, but don't feel guilty if you leave them at home. Don't forget, they have each other.

Chapter 8 will address another problem common to multiple-dog owners—taking vacations. This is something else that can cause guilt or even resentment among multiple-dog owners. By using some of the suggestions and ideas in the next chapter, you will be able to get away with or without your dogs and come back home refreshed.

FURTHER REFERENCE

Therapy Dogs, Inc.
2416 East Fox Farm Road
Cheyenne, WY 82007

North American Flyball Association
1342 Jeff St.
Ypsilanti, MI 48198

United States Dog Agility Association
P.O. Box 850955
Richarson, TX 75085-0955

Carting Informatiom Packet
Newfoundland Club of America
Roger Powell - Working Dog Committee
5808 Olive Rd.
Raleigh, NC 27606

SUGGESTED READING

Morgan, Lonnie. *Flyball: A Sport For Everyone.* 1990

Schwartz, Charlotte. *Friend to Friend: Dog'sThat Help Mankind.* Howell Book House, New York, NY. 1984

Kohl and Goldstein. *The All Breed Dog Grooming Guide.* Prentice Hall Press, New York, NY. 1987

Pearsall, Milo D. *Scent Training to Track, Search, and Rescue.* Alpine Press, Loveland, CO. 1982

Gallup, Davia Anne. *Running with Man's Best Friend.* Alpine Press, Loveland, CO

Flanders, Noel. *The Joy of Running Sled Dogs.* Alpine Press, Loveland, CO. 1989

Milon, Ellie. *201 Ways to Enjoy Your Dog, A Complete Guide to Organized U.S. and Canadian Activities for Dog Lovers.* Alpine Press, CO. 1990

Chapter Eight
VACATIONING

At one time or another, most folks need to get away. It might be to escape the stress of your job, or a family emergency might be the reason you need to be away from home. Whatever the reason, once you have multiple dogs, it takes a little more planning to leave home. But it certainly is not impossible.

Two things surprised me when I was initially reading the questionnaires:

1. The number of people who no longer vacationed because they had multiple dogs.
2. The number of people who vacationed with their dogs. Even people who own five or more dogs took their dogs with them.

I had to wonder how you get from not vacationing at all to enjoying time away from home with or without all of your dogs. This chapter will share with you all of the information you will need to plan for a vacation or be prepared for an emergency that will call you away from home.

As you read this chapter, you might find that not all of your dogs can cope with each of these suggestions. You might have to bring a couple of the dogs to the kennel, bring one dog over to friend, or get a pet sitter for the two left at home. When we go away, we like taking along one or two dogs, if possible. My parents' home is small, so if we take the big dogs when we visit them, we board them at a close-by kennel we all like. We can check the dogs out for walks or a run on the beach. This works out well for us. Depending on the availability of our pet sitter, who stays at the house, we will leave a couple of the dogs at home. We try to mix and match and rotate who comes and who stays at home. So read on and decide which options will work for you and your dogs.

OPTIONS

Some dogs are more comfortable at home than traveling. Your options for keeping your dogs at home while you are away are:

- Get a neighbor to come over to feed, exercise, and clean up after your dogs.
- Have family members, such as grown children, ex-spouses, in-laws, or brothers or sisters attend to the daily tasks.
- Hire a pet sitter that will stop by two to four times a day.
- Hire a pet sitter that lives in your home during your absence.

A

Friend in Need...

Your neighbors can be a godsend for many reasons, but nothing is as special as a neighbor who will watch your dogs for you. This option seems to be the first choice for most people. It works out best if the neighbor has dogs; then you can repay the favor by watching their dogs. Even if your neighbors are unable to watch your dogs while you are away, they can monitor the arrangements you have made. One respondent wrote that her dogs were barking excessively at night while she was away. The neighbor came over and watched a little TV with the dogs each night, and the problem was solved.

Dear Uncle Joe

If you are lucky enough to live near your family, you probably have someone who would either stay at your house or take the dogs into his or her home. Today, with all the members in extended families, this choice provides lots of options. Ex-spouses are a popular choice because they are usually familiar with the dogs and seem to enjoy the time with them.

Pet Sitters

If you don't already know someone reliable who can stop by or stay at your house, you will need to hire someone. Most pet sitters charge by the visit and will stop by as often as you need them. If you live in a small community, you probably know some-one who knows someone who does pet sitting. If that is not the case, you will need to contact a professional service. You can get the name of a reliable service through word-of-mouth or from your groomer, veterinarian, animal shelter, or an ad on a bulletin board or in the paper. Check references of anyone you are going to en-trust with the care of your dogs and your home. The pet sitter should stop by sometime prior to your departure to meet the dogs and find out where the food, leashes, and cleaning supplies for house and yard are, and what the emergency phone numbers are.

Plan ahead and you could have the sitter come a few times before your leave on your big trip. If you are going to work late, have the sitter stop by and let the dogs out at noon for a breath of fresh air, exercise, and a chance to get used to a stranger in the house. This will give you some idea of the reliability of the sitter and put your mind to rest. You will then also be prepared for an emergency that could call you away from home. With one phone call to your pet sitter, you will know your dogs are taken care of, and you can take care of the business at hand.

Be aware that some dogs do not like to stay at home without someone in the home with them. As you can imagine, if the nor-mal pattern in your home is a lot of activity and all of a sudden the dogs are left alone day and night, it can be stressful for your dogs. This can cause housebreaking mistakes or other destructive be-haviors that your dogs would not normally consider. If this is your situation, you need to find a pet sitter that will stay overnight. Look for a service that offers this choice, but be sure they are bonded and insured.

Hide the Rawhides, Here Comes Spot for the Weekend

Another option is finding someone who will take your dogs into their home. I'm such a "someone." Dogs come and stay with us in our home while the owners are away. The first day or so is always interesting if the dogs have not been here before. Generally, by the time the dogs go home, they have enjoyed their stay, and the next time they come, it is like old home week. This works out well, especially if the dogs are crate-trained. But even if the dogs don't use a crate at home, most of them feel comfortable in one here. We keep the crates in our family room, so the visiting dogs are not isolated.

The Country Club

You might also consider boarding your dogs at a boarding kennel, with the breeder from whom you got your dog, or with your veterinarian. If this is the option that you choose, remember, some kennels are nicer than others. If you decide to board at your veterinarian, make sure the healthy dogs are kept separate from the dogs that are there because they are sick. Be sure to visit the kennel before you take your dogs there. If you are not allowed to inspect the kennel area, forget that one and go to the next one on your list. Look for cleanliness, watch how kennel attendants interact with the dogs they handle, and make sure the size of the runs is large enough for your dogs' comfort. Drains should be working, and the air should not be foul smelling. If this basic criteria is not met, move on to the next facility. Having a kennel chosen before you need it will prepare you for any unexpected trips you will need to take.

A reputable kennel will insist that your dogs' vaccinations are current. This should include a vaccine to prevent "kennel cough," or bordatella. Kennel cough is a respiratory infection that is highly infectious. A characteristic sign of this illness is a harsh, dry cough. The name comes from the fact that while being boarded at a kennel, your dog is exposed to other dogs that have the disease or are carriers of it. Although the bordatella vaccine is not complete protection against kennel cough, it does protect against 90 percent of the cases of kennel cough.

FRIENDLY
KENNELS

    Besides requiring current vaccinations, the kennel should also request the name and phone number of your veterinarian and your emergency numbers. You should also ask the kennel owner about their emergency plans just in case there is a fire, flood, or earthquake while you are away. If your dogs are on special diets, the kennel should be happy to accommodate those needs. A nicety would be bringing your dogs' bedding from home and having it laundered regularly during their stay. Make sure anything you leave with your dogs is properly labeled. Some kennels will allow your dogs to share a run, which is nice if your dogs are buddies. Another thing to ask about is whether your dogs will have a chance to get together in a fenced play area. This play time should be supervised, and only include your dogs.
    Cleanliness and quality of care during your dogs stay are the keys to a good kennel. In urban areas, the kennel runs may be more cramped than a kennel that is located in the country. If the attendants visit and handle the dogs regularly throughout the day

and keep the runs clean, your dogs will be fine. To end your dogs' stay at the kennel, have them bathed, so when they get home, they are fresh, clean, flea-free, and ready for hugs and kisses.

DOGS' ACTIVITIES

Now for the fun part, taking your dogs with you when you travel. This takes as much responsibility as finding a good pet sitter or boarding kennel. It also depends on the type of trip you are taking. A trip in the middle of summer to a place where the weather is hot and where you are planning on a lot of sightseeing side trips is not a trip most dogs would enjoy. You would be doing your dogs a favor leaving them at home. To successfully vacation with your dogs, the trip needs to include activities that include your dog such as hiking, swimming, or relaxing in the shade.

WHO AM I?

To travel safely with your dogs, you need to make sure each dog has proper identification. You should look for the sort of ID tag that lets you easily change the information. When you get to the new location, you can change the information to include the hotel or campground where you are that night. Make sure your dogs wear their rabies tags. The rabies tag should have the name and phone number of your veterinarian on it. If the only tag your dog has on is one with your home address and phone number, you could run into some trouble. When the person who finds your dog tries to contact you, you won't be home.

WHAT TO BRING

Your dogs will need you to pack for them, too. Remember to bring food, dishes, crate, toys, bedding (that can be easily washed), bug and flea spray, and health documents. Stop by your veterinarian for a health certificate that will verify your dogs' good health and vaccinations. A health certificate may be required in some states and by some motels. If for some reason you unexpectantly need to kennel your dogs, you'll have the necessary paperwork to do it with the minimum amount of hassle. The pre-trip visit will also inform your vet and staff that you will be traveling with your dogs. Bring along a snapshot and description of each dog to be used just in case one of your dogs does get lost.

DON'T DRINK THE WATER

While you are visiting with your veterinarian, ask about any diseases that might be prevalent in the area where you are traveling. For instance, we don't have heartworm where we live, but we were traveling to an area of the country where it was common. We were careful to use bug spray when the dogs weren't in the motor home, and we gave heartworm medicine for a prescribed time when we got home.

GET OUT THE GUIDE BOOK

You've made all the pretravel preparations, now where should you go? Visiting friends who are also dog lovers is probably the easiest and most fun. Your friends with dogs will already know the best places to walk dogs, where the dog-friendly beaches are, and will most likely have a secured fenced yard. We have some special friends whom we visit regularly with our dogs. It is an eight-hour drive to their house. We all enjoy that time in the car being close with the dogs. The dogs remember each other from past visits and are playing together before we get the car unpacked. If we ever go visit without the dogs, when we get home we get sniffed up and down. I'm sure our dogs can smell their pals and wonder why we got away and they had to stay home.

The Great Outdoors

Camping is another way to travel with your dogs. Most campgrounds allow dogs. You will need to keep your dogs on leash, control their barking, and clean up after them. These seem like things any responsible dog owner would do without being told, but if you go anywhere people have been with their dogs, you'll find piles of dog waste that have been ignored by the dogs' owner. Nothing is worse than seeing or stepping in dog poop, except maybe sitting in it. This is probably the most common reason why dogs are not welcome everywhere.

There are many different ways to go camping. You can camp in the wilderness, at national parks, or at independently owned campgrounds. You can sleep in tents, travel by motor home, or pull a camper. If you are going far from home, you will need some type of campground guide book that will let you know where dogs are allowed. Look at the end of this chapter for a list of books that can help. It is, however, always a good idea to call ahead just to make sure policy hasn't changed. When camping closer to home, you can ask friends who camp with dogs where they go. Word-of-mouth is an invaluable tool for those of us who have multiple dogs.

Pet Motels

If your trip involves driving a long distance, you may have to stay in motels while on the road. Again, this will take some research. Prudent travelers will call ahead to check the dog policy, make reservations, and plan their stops. If you can't find a motel that allows dogs and you are only staying one night, it is possible to have the dogs sleep in their crates in the car. With the extra walks the dogs have been getting and the time you have spent together in the car, a day on vacation still beats a day when you are gone all day at work, or being left behind.

Club Dog

Many multiple-dog owners have found wonderful resorts that allow dogs. These locations are the hot destinations for yearly vacations with the dogs. Without getting specific, but rather to let you know wonderful dog-friendly resorts do exist, here is a sampling of some of the places that multiple-dog families like to go:

- In Tennessee, a log cabin on five acres
- A beach resort in Florida that caters to dogs who bring their owners
- A lovely hotel in Nevada, right on a river
- In Maryland, a beach house that allows dogs for a fee
- A gorgeous waterfront home in North Carolina with a dog-friendly policy

Camps

Another idea for vacationing with your dogs is camps that are specifically designed for dogs and their owners. Camps of this sort are becoming more popular and sound like a lot of fun. Generally, for a set fee, the camp includes room, board, and activities for you and your dogs. (Two dogs per person seems to be the limit.) The activities might include seminars with professional trainers to help you with problems, show you how to teach your dogs to play games like flyball, and get you started with tracking, carting, or herding with your dogs. At the end of this chapter, I will include the names of three camps that were sent to me by respondents.

The Show Circuit

People who travel to dog shows regularly pack up dogs and supplies and head out for the weekend without it being a big ordeal. How do they manage that? Practice makes perfect. Show folks also know that most motels do have certain rooms set aside for people with dogs. Since I belong to the Newfoundland Club of Seattle, I spoke to folks who travel with Newfs. I was assured that they were seldom turned away from motels.

In one instance, the dog show was on the East Coast. After the show, the family stayed on the East Coast for a two-week vacation and had no problem finding motels that accepted dogs. There was also no problem renting a car. Some travel tips were suggested:

- Have the food packaged per day in zip-lock bags. If your dog is used to canned food mixed with the dry, use the small pop-top can so you will not have to deal with opened cans of dog food while on the road.

- Don't stop at restaurants for your meals as the dogs will have to wait in the car and that can be dangerous. Instead, pack a picnic, and eat at rest areas so the dogs can get out of the car with you.

Bon Voyage.

I hope those of you who haven't yet traveled with your dogs will give it a try. Never feel guilty about leaving your dogs behind either. If you do your leg work and find the best kennel or a pet sitter your dogs like, their time without you will be stress-free.

For more information on dog camps, write to one of these folks:

Camp Gone to the Dogs
Honey Loring
RR 1
Putney, VT 05346

Supercamp
Canine Behavior Services
83 Gilhaven Road
Manchester, NH 03104

Behavior and Training Camps
Terry Ryan
NW 2025 Friel Street
Pullman, WA 99163

Books to order:

Touring With Touser
Quaker Professional Services
585 Hawthorne Court
Galesburg, IL 61401
$3.00

Pets on the Go
Alpo Pet Foods
P.O. Box 25200
Leigh Valley, PA 18002-5200
Free, SASE

SUGGESTED READING

Pets Permitted Hotel and Motel Directory, 93/94 Edition

or

On the Road Again With Man's Best Friend
New England Edition
West Coast Edition

Chapter Nine
GROUP HEALTH

Maintaining your dogs' health is one of the biggest expenses (food is the biggest and an integral part of your dogs health) of a multiple-dog owner. This chapter describes the steps you should take to select a veterinarian, followed by some suggestions of things you can do to avoid going to the veterinarian. When you own multiple dogs, you will not be able to totally avoid trips to the veterinarian, so this chapter describes some criteria for determining whether a visit is necessary.

You may decide to try an alternative method of treatment for your dogs. Some alternatives include chiropractic, massage, herbal remedies, or homeopathy. A brief description of each of these choices is also included in this chapter.

DOING YOUR HOMEWORK

Don't wait until one of your dogs is sick to find a veterinarian. The first place to look is in the phone book to see what is available in your area. If you work full-time Monday through Friday and only one vet in your area is open evenings, you can start by visiting that office. Go unannounced one evening, and check out the lobby area first. You can tell a lot about a place by observing the receptionist. Listen to how he/she is answering the phone.

Is she/he polite, interested, and efficient? Do you see any diplomas on the wall? Is the veterinarian a member of the American Veterinary Medical Association (AVMA)? To be a member of this professional organization, the veterinarian must have graduated from an accredited school.

While checking out the office, assuming you like what you see so far, make an appointment to bring one of your dogs in for a basic physical. This initial visit will give you an idea of this veterinarian's feelings about dogs. You will be able to see if the doctor can handle the dog competently and with concern. Have a list of questions that you know the answers to already prepared. Is the doctor patronizing, or is he or she really interested in helping you and your dog? If you are not satisfied at any point during this initial consultation, go to the next name on your list.

Most multiple-dog owners admit to spending more money at the vet's on their dogs' health care than on their own.. If things have gone well and you are happy with what you have seen so far, admit to being a multiple-dog owner, and ask about a multiple-dog discount. Every little bit helps, and most veterinarians are will ing to give some sort of discount, especially if you bring more than one dog in with you at the time of your visits. It will also be very helpful to your new vet if you have your dogs' records from your previous veterinarian.

If you live in a big city, there are probably 24-hour emergency clinics you can go to if you have a problem on a Sunday or late at night. In small communities this is often not the case, so ask about how your veterinarian will cover that type of situation. We all know that most emergencies happen when it is least convenient!

The above advice assumes you have relocated to a new city or town. If you have become dissatisfied with your present doctor, you can follow the same advice. If you are not relocating, you will have the advantage of word-of-mouth from other multiple-dog owners you already know. When you are new to a community, you don't have that luxury. A good way to meet dog lovers in your new community and to get to know the veterinarians is to volunteer at the local animal shelter.

HEALTHINESS IS NEXT TO GODLINESS

Now that you have found a veterinarian, you want to try to avoid going to see him or her. Maintaining your dogs' health is the way to do that.

Dogs Are What They Eat

First, feed your dogs a good quality, nutritious dog food. This type of dog food will cost more up front, but it will save you money in the long run. Once you've found the right food, don't overfeed your dogs. An overweight dog may have some serious health problems to deal with, such as, arthritis, joint injuries, diabetes, pancreatitis, and a shortened life expectancy. To determine whether your dog is overweight, feel for its ribs. You should be able to feel the dog's ribs without pressing hard. If all you feel is fat, your dog should start eating less and exercising more.

The Future Belongs to the Fit

An exercise schedule appropriate for your dogs' ages will keep them healthy and away from the doctor's office. Multiple-dog families have the advantage over single-dog families because the dogs generally keep each other in pretty good shape. For some ideas about exercises for your dogs, check out Chapter 7.

Brush after Every Meal

A healthy dog will have clean teeth and gums. This can be accomplished by cleaning their teeth regularly. Twice a week will generally do the trick. Most dogs don't care for the taste of human tooth paste; in fact, it can make some dogs vomit. It is worth the investment to get toothpaste made especially for dogs. The dogs like the taste, so that makes it easier for them to tolerate the cleaning. Before you start using a toothbrush on your dogs, put the toothpaste on your gauze-wrapped finger, and rub the teeth and gums.

Gradually work your way up to the use of a toothbrush.

Avoid a diet based mostly of canned or semimoist foods because they lack the abrasive action needed for healthy teeth and gums. This type of food might also be high in sugars (read the labels). Dry food, along with safe, hard chew-toys for your dogs, helps maintain healthy gums.

Closing Down the Flea Circus

Try to maintain a flea-free environment for the health of your dogs. In some areas of the country, fleas are only a seasonal problem because of the cold winters. In hot and humid areas, the conditions are perfect for fleas and they can multiply quickly. In these areas, fleas are a problem all year. One of the causes of tapeworms is fleas. Fleas feed on the blood of their host (the host can be a dog, cat, squirrel, opossum, or HUMAN—anything with warm blood) and cause anemia.

To determine whether your dogs have fleas, look at the base of the tail or roll the dog over and take a look at the tummy. If there are fleas, you should see little black flecks on your dog's skin. These flecks are "flea dirt," which is really blood-filled flea excrement. A drop of water on flea dirt will turn it into a red fluid. Once you have determined your dogs have fleas, it will take some work to bring the problem under control.

The basics of flea control start with bathing all your animals with an effective flea shampoo, following the directions on the product. This may have to be done once a week or even more often than that to get the problem under control. Once the fleas are gone, an effective repellent is a rinse of Avon's Skin-So-Soft™ bath oil (1.5 ounces of Skin-So-Soft mixed with one gallon of water). This is not a proven method, but I read the suggestion enough times not to overlook it.

I don't recommend flea dips that are left on the dog and not rinsed off. Every time you or anyone in your family pets your dogs, they are touching the flea dip. If any of your dogs groom each other, or if you have cats that play with your dogs, they will ingest the flea dip. Unless you wash your hands after each time you touch your dogs, you might end up ingesting some flea dip yourself.

Another type of flea control you might want to avoid are the systemic poisons recommended by some veterinarian. These poisons are either taken by your dog in pill form or are applied to your dog's skin and absorbed into his blood stream. The disadvantages are these:

1. You are feeding your dog poison (or applying poison to his skin).
2. The fleas still bite your dog. They have to bite the dog and ingest blood to be poisoned.

There is a new drug Lufenuron (Program) which is safe, effective, and not harmful to the environment. When the female flea bites a dog taking this drug, her eggs are unable to hatch, thus breaking the flea life cycle. Ask your veterinarian for more information.

Along with bathing all your pets, you need to wash the pets' bedding and spray the areas in your home where your animals spend a lot of time. When the problem is severe, you might even have to spray the outdoor areas where your pets hang out. When choosing the products you will use in the war against fleas, keep in mind the environment as well as the health of your animals. Ask your veterinarian for advice, and read all the directions on the products you choose.

My best defense against fleas is vacuuming everyday. After you vacuum, you should empty your vacuum bag into your outdoor garbage container to keep the fleas from crawling out of the vacuum and back into your house. The idea of putting a section of flea collar into your vacuum is not an environmentally sound idea. As you are vacuuming, you may be releasing pesticides into the air.

Spraying your carpets every two weeks is another line of defense. Since flea larvae like dark areas make sure you spray under the furniture as well. I also wash all of the throw rugs once a week.

The carpet sprays are more effective for fleas than the insect bombs, since the mist from the bombs doesn't go under the furniture or around corners.

Shoot the Dog

Another aspect of maintaining good health and contributing to a longer life for your dogs is keeping them properly vaccinated. What diseases do you need to vaccinate against?

Canine distemper is a highly contagious viral disease that is often fatal. Distemper can live for years in a frozen state and is present wherever there are susceptible animals. The overall health of a dog exposed to the virus has a lot to do with whether the dog actually contracts the disease, and if he does, the seriousness of the case.

Hepatitis in dogs should not be confused with hepatitis in humans. Infectious canine hepatitis is sometimes difficult to distinguish from distemper. This disease is spread from contact with an infected dog, its urine, stool, or saliva.

Leptospirosis is a disease in dogs that can be spread to humans. The disease is spread in the urine of infected animals. Rats are one of the main carriers, and cattle can also be an important source. The bacteria enters through breaks in the skin, or through drinking or eating food contaminated by infected urine. This disease can cause chronic kidney problems.

Parainfluenza is one of the germs involved in "kennel cough." Although parainfluenza is often mild in healthy dogs, it is highly contagious and can be severe in puppies or dogs in poor health.

Bordetella can also be a contributor to kennel cough.

Parvovirus attacks the gastrointestinal tract, causing vomiting and diarrhea. It can also affect bone marrow, lymph nodes, and the heart. It is transmitted from one dog to another through contaminated saliva and feces. Dogs and humans can carry the disease on their hair and feet. This virus is extremely hardy and can resist most household cleaners. It can also surivive for years in the environment. However, chlorine bleach is effective in killing parvo on surfaces like floors, crates, etc.

Corona virus is another highly contagious disease of the intestine causing diarrhea and vomiting. Dehydration from this disease can be life threatening.

Rabies is a fatal disease that occurs in warm-blooded animals and is transmitted through bites and exposure to an infected animal. The rabies virus attacks the brain and the central nervous system. Any wild animal that allows you or your dogs to approach should be suspected as a rabies carrier. *There is no effective treatment for infected dogs.* Keep your dogs' rabies vaccinations current.

Lyme disease is caused by a bacteria transmitted to dogs, cats, and humans mainly by ticks. This disease, most commonly exhibted by shifting-leg lameness/arthritis, can lead to paralysis, seizures, fever, and even death. Prevention through vaccination is now an option, or you may choose to use a tick collar that will make the ticks detach before they inject the Lyme organism. Prevention is also possible without vaccination with good grooming and envi ronmental tick control, such as keeping the grass, weeds, and brush cut short. If your dog does get Lyme disease, it is treatable with an antibiotic therapy.

What should you do if you do find a tick on your dog? Remove IT! First, kill the tick by applying alcohol or fingernail polish directly on the tick with a cotton-tipped applicator. The tick will die in a few moments, then you should grasp it with tweezers as close to the skin as you can get and slowly pull it out. Do not use your fingers in the removal of the tick, because if you had a cut on your finger and the tick is engorged, you could end up with lyme disease. Do not be concerned if the head stays with the dog; keep an eye on the location; it should clear up in a few days. If your dog has a lot of ticks, you would do best to contact your veterinarian for treatment advise.

Heartworm disease is transmitted from infected dogs to noninfected dogs by mosquitoes. Once injected by the infected mosquito, the immature worms (microfilaria) travel to the heart and become adults. This trip from immature worm to adulthood takes about six months. The mature worms reproduce, and the immature worms circulate through the bloodstream where they are picked up by mosquitoes and transferred to other dogs. The treatment for heartworm can be lengthy, expensive, and dangerous. It involves injecting the dog with a poison to kill the worms. The poison is an arsenic compound which is hard on your dog's liver, so make sure your dog is strong enough to withstand therapy. Often, the lungs and heart become congested with the dead worms, and that can cause death, too. Again, prevention is your best avenue of defense. Before you start prevention, make sure your dog is not already infected with microfilaria with a blood test performed by your veterinarian. However, if your dog is less than 6 months old, it can generally go directly on medication. This is usually done with tablets given everyday or once a month, depending on the type of preventative tablet prescribed by your vet. You will start giving the prevention one month before mosquito season starts and will stop sixty days after it is over. (In some areas of the country, you may need to give the preventative all year long.)

The importance of keeping your dogs properly vaccinated should not be overlooked, especially if your dogs routinely come in contact with dogs or the feces of dogs with whom you are not familiar. All of these diseases are highly contagious and can spread through your house or kennel before you can stop them. Although vaccines cannot guarantee that your dogs will not get sick, they certainly give you an advantage. Most vaccines require a yearly booster to keep your dogs protected. Revaccinating every six months for dogs that go to shows, are boarded, or whose owners volunteer at shelters is prudent and provides the surest protection for your dogs.

Most states have laws requiring rabies vaccinations to be given by a licensed veterinarian. Other vaccines can be given by your veterinarian or at home by you. If you decide to give the vaccines yourself, you can purchase the vaccines from your veterinarian, a catalog, or many feed stores. You must make sure the vaccines have been properly handled, no matter where you have acquired them. They must be refrigerated during transportation and prior to use, actually refrigerated at all times, and you should check the expiration date. Always keep accurate records of the date you administered the vaccine. Include in those records the name and lot number of the vaccine administered.

Your veterinarian may or may not help you get started in this endeavor. A responsible dog owner is just as capable of proper handling of vaccines as a veterinarian's office. Most veterinary hospitals get their vaccines through the mail and are also trusting the reputation of the vaccine producer and the delivery company. But giving vaccines to dogs is a big money-maker for veterinary clinics. Quite a few veterinarians around the country realize that multiple-dog owners couldn't manage without the vet's expertise in many areas such as diagnostics, X-rays, or surgery, and they are willing to help the owner get started on vaccinating their own dogs. Vaccinating is something multiple-dog owners can do on their own that can reduce the cost of dog ownership.

Only healthy dogs should be vaccinated, so quickly take your dog's temperature before administering the vaccine. Although just taking the temperature does not insure that your dog is healthy, it is one of the indicators. You should also be aware of your dogs' stools and general well-being. If your dog is listless, won't eat, etc., hold off on the vaccinating, and plan a trip to the doctor. The procedure for taking your dog's temperature is described later in this chapter. When we vaccinate our dogs, I space out the vaccines so we don't give them all at once. For example, we administer the bordetella one week, being careful to watch for any reaction. Then we give the distemper, hepatitis, leptospirosis, parainfluenza, and parvovirus (this is generally one vaccine, called DHLPP) the next week. This way, the dog's immune system has time to adjust to each vaccine. If you are vaccinating puppies you should give the booster shots every three weeks for the best immune response.

This does not diminish the importance of a thorough yearly physical for your dogs. Veterinarian Kellee Roberti, D.V.M. adds that it is surprising how often diseases are detected during the rou tine yearly physical. Keep in mind that most veterinarians give a group discount if you bring all your dogs in at once. Another option is having your veterinarian make a house call to check on all of your dogs at once.

Mom, My Tummy Hurts

There will be many times when you will need to bring your dogs to see the veterinarian. What are some of the signs that indicate a visit?

Diarrhea can be a sign of illness if it lasts more than a day or two, has blood in it, or is accompanied by a fever. When you own multiple dogs, it may be difficult to determine which dog has the diarrhea. When you feed the dogs their next meal, grate a different color crayon in each dog dish. When your dogs have their next stool you can tell which dog has the problem.

Vomiting occasionally occurs in most dogs and is not a disease but a symptom of other problems. If your dog seems healthy at all other times, you probably don't need to worry, but if the vomiting persists or is bloody, take the dog in for an examination. If your dog seems distressed in any way call your veterinarian. Vomiting can be a sign of an obstruction, poisoning, tumors, or other sources of illness.

Your dog's temperature is a good indicator of whether something is wrong. The normal temperature for a dog is 101.3° F, although it can range from 100° F to 102.5° F. Taking your dog's temperature is an easy procedure and is done by inserting the thermometer in the dog's rectum. Here are the steps:

- Shake the thermometer down to the 96° F range.
- Lubricate the thermometer bulb with vaseline for easy insertion.
- It is usually easiest to have the dog lay on its side for this procedure, but it can also be done with the dog standing.
- Insert the thermometer into the dog's rectum with a twisting

motion, one to three inches is far enough, and leave it in for one minute.
- Remove the thermometer, wipe it off if you need to, and read the temperature.
- Clean the thermometer with alcohol before using it again.

Other indicators that your dog may need to see the veterinarian are lack of appetite, no energy, or a change in normal daily habits. If you are new to multiple-dog ownership, you should read one or more of the books at the end of this chapter. You will gain knowledge as your experience with dogs grows. If you are ever in doubt, make the appointment. Whenever I take a dog to see the veterinarian, I try to learn something new to expand my knowledge about dogs.

DAMAGE CONTROL

As a multiple-dog owner, there are some common health problems you will probably encounter at one time or another.

Allergies are a problem for dogs and can be caused by insect bites, certain foods, pollen, and many other things too numerous to list here. An allergic reaction will cause the dog to scratch, sneeze, cough, vomit, or have diarrhea. Canine allergies are one of the main causes of problems with your dogs' skin.

Arthritis is a buildup of a bone-like material in areas such as on a bone or joint surface. X-rays are the best way to confirm that your dog has arthritis. Wear and tear on the joints over the course of the lifetime may cause this disease. If you notice your dog having a hard time getting up in the morning or after a nap, and if you see a general stiffness that worsens in the cold weather, your dog might have arthritis.

Ear infections can be very frustrating to treat. Your veterinarian will be able to tell you whether it is a bacterial or yeast infection. If you notice your dog shaking his head or scratching at his ears, or if his ears look red on the inside or have an offensive odor, a trip to the vet is in order.

Hip dysplasia is a problem in the structure of the hip joint. The ball and socket of the hip should fit together snugly. If that is not the case and the joint is too loose, there will be excessive movement. Over time, the excessive movement causes extra bone to form, creating the additional problem of arthritis. Hip dysplasia is usually inherited and is common among littermates whose parents have the disease, although nondysplastic parents can have puppies with dysplasia. Dysplasia can also be aggravated by injury, obesity, or excessive stressful motion repeated over a long period of time (like jumping on and off a dog house, all day, every day, for years). The Orthopedic Foundation for Animals (OFA) certifies purebred dogs over the age of two years by viewing X-rays of their hips. This certification verifies whether the dog is free of hip dysplasia, and if is not, the degree to which the hips are affected.

Urine leakage is most common in older spayed female dogs that suffer from a lack of the hormone estrogen. Often, supplementing the dog with the estrogen hormone can eliminate the problem. Make sure however that you have an urinalysis done before you assume it is low estogen that is causing the problems. It could also be a bladder infection, so once again a trip to your veterinarian is in order.

Internal Parasites come in many varieties. The most common ones for dogs are roundworms and tapeworms.

Roundworms look like strands of spaghetti that move. You will find them in the dogs' stools or vomit. You can prevent roundworms by practicing good sanitation (i.e., clean up after your dog!). Roundworms enter the dogs orally, in the egg stage, from the ground and hatch in the dog's intestine. From there the larvae travel through the bloodstream into the lungs. Once in the lungs, the larvae become mobile and crawl up the windpipe and are swallowed. Then it is back to the intestine to develop into an adult. Puppies are more susceptible to roundworms than adults. In adult dogs only a few larvae return to the intestine, the others remain dormant. If the adult dog is pregnant, the dormant larvae are released during the last stages of pregnancy, reenter circulation, and are carried to the unborn puppies. Puppies can also get circulating larvae through breast milk.

Tapeworms are usually spread among dogs through fleas. A tapeworm develops after the dog has eaten an infected flea. Tapeworms look like pieces of rice and are found in the feces. You prevent tapeworms by controlling fleas.

You can control both of these types of worms by

- Not letting your dogs run free and have access to dead animals.
- Not feeding your dogs raw meat or uncooked game.
- Having your dogs' stools checked for parasites by your veterinarian twice a year.
- Removing stools from your dog's exercise area everyday.
- Getting rid of pests such as fleas, lice, mice, and other rodents all of whom are intermediate hosts for tapeworms.
- Keeping your dogs from eating the feces of other animals (e.g., rabbit pellets).

External Parasites include fleas and ticks, which we have already covered. Two types of mites are also worth mentioning: the sarcoptic mange mite and the demodectic mange mite.

Sarcoptic Mange causes skin irritation which will make your dog scratch and bite itself. This type of mange is highly contagious, making it the most common type found on dogs. A skin scraping or a biopsy is needed for a diagnosis; then you will be able to start treatment. The treatment involves dipping your dogs at least three times, ten days apart, in an insecticide dip.

Demodectic Mange is caused by a microscopic, cigar-shaped mite and is the most serious and difficult to treat. All dogs are susceptible to it ,and most dogs harbor the parasite in the skin. The parasite is a harmless resident on the skin. It is only a problem when the mites begin reproducing at a high rate, which they do when the dog's immune system is compromised. There are also indications that genetic and hereditary factors are important. Demodectic mange comes in two varieties, generalized and localized. The localized form may or may not be itchy and is normally seen as small patches. This type is self-limiting, responds well to treatment, and in most cases will go away on its own. The generalized cases are stubborn, resistant conditions that do not respond well to treatment. The hair loss can be severe, with the skin becoming red and inflamed. Again, skin scrapings or a biopsy are needed for an accurate diagnosis.

DIFFERENT STROKES

Every dog owner should also be aware of the alternative methods of health care available for dogs. You might decide to use an alternative method of treatment when you have tried all the suggestions of traditional veterinary medicine. You might also have found success at the chiropractor or with acupuncture and want to try the same drug-free treatments for your dogs. Whatever your reasons, acupuncture, chiropractic, and holistic methods are being accepted and used by many veterinarians around the country.

Stick 'em Up

Acupuncture is an ancient healing art that is steadily being incorporated into veterinary medicine. The decision to use acupuncture should depend on the type of disease your dog has. It would not be appropriate to use acupuncture to cure a bacterial infection, although it would be appropriate for help with arthritis. In dogs, problems involving pain, paralysis, and allergies are the most common uses for acupuncture.

Acupuncture is the insertion of needles into specific points. Once the needles are inserted, they might be twirled by hand before removal or left alone. The needles come in different sizes, and the size and depth of insertion depend on the size of the patient. In modern veterinary acupuncture electricity is sometimes used to stimulate the needles with dramatic results.

When looking for a veterinary acupuncturist, first make sure the person is a licensed veterinarian. Then make sure he or she is formally trained to use acupuncture on animals. Your state Veteri narian Association should be able to help you locate a veterinarian who practices acupunture. Acupuncture works well for a variety of ailments in dogs. Whether it works or fails, side effects are very rare.

Body Work

Chiropractic adjustments keep the body in balance, from the bones to the immune system. Chiropractic adjustments encourage the body to heal itself through adjustments and manipulation of various body parts, mainly the spinal column. The theory is that all disease is traceable to nervous system malfunctions usually caused by misalignment of the spinal column. Treatments might be limited to two or three visits, or they might require a longer series of visits. The maintenance treatments might require visits once a month or maybe only annual checkups.

Chiropractic is a non-invasive treatment, so if the dog does not improve, nothing harmful has occurred. Chiropractic can lengthen your dogs' lives and relieve any pain they may be suffer ing. This sort of treatment is not recognized by the American Veterinarian Medical Association.

Heal Yourself

Homeopathy is a system of medicine that stimulates the body's defense system, allowing the body to heal itself. Homeopathic remedies consist of "drugs" that are diluted many times. Homeopathic "drugs" can be things like injecting minute amounts of a substance to which a dog is allergic in order to stimulate the immune system to produce antibodies to that substance. The dilutions are done in a specific manner, and the more diluted the medicine is, the stronger the potency. Because the homeopathic remedies are prescribed in such small doses, they are nontoxic and have no side effects. However, due to the nature of homeopathic remedies, the dog often appears to get worse before he gets better.

Chiropractic, acupuncture, and homeopathy, can all be used in conjunction with traditional veterinary medicine. For more information on the alternative methods of care for your dogs, write to the addresses that are listed here.

To locate an alternative veterinarian in your area, write or call one of the following:

American Holistic Veterinary Medical Association
2214 Old Emmorton Road
Bel Air, MD 21014
(301) 638-0385

International Veterinary Acupuncture Society
Meredith L. Snader, V.M.D., Executive Director
2140 Conestoga Road
Chester Springs, PA 19425
(215) 827-7245

National Center for Homeopathy
801 N. Fairfax #306
Alexandria, VA 22314
(703) 548-7790

SUGGESTED READING

Brennan D.V.M., Mary L. *The Natural Dog*. PLUME, New York, NY. 1993

Carlson and Giffin. *Dog Owner's Home Veterinary Handbook*. Howell Book House, New York, NY. 1980

Stein, Diane. *Natural Healing for Dogs and Cats*. The Crossing Press, Freedom, CA. 1993

Various Authors. *Merck Veterinary Manual*. Merck & Co., Inc. Rahay, N.J. 1991

Chapter Ten
THE GOLDEN YEARS AND BEYOND

This final chapter is about a subject that all dog owners wish we didn't have to face. When you own multiple dogs, you will have to face it over and over. Believe me, it doesn't get easier. All of our dogs will get old, and they all will eventually die. Hopefully, it will happen in that order. This chapter looks at older dogs and suggests things you can do to make their last years as comfortable as possible. After you have done everything you can to make your dogs' golden years special, and when the time has finally come for your dog to die at home, or for you to make the tough decision about euthanasia, you will have to decide what to do with the body. Through the questionnaires, I discovered there are many ways to remember your four-legged companions that have died. These real-life situations will give you some idea of the possibilities available and help you with the decisions that need to be made.

THE END OF AN ERA

First, let's take a look at some of the considerations that might be needed with older dogs. The oldest dog in the pack is generally the alpha dog. This can cause a problem when the younger dogs start to see the older dog lose some of his power. This loss of power can mean a loss of pride for the older dog.

Most youngsters with an alpha attitude could not only damage the pride of a senior dog but could also physically harm him. If dogs lived without humans in their packs, the older alpha would be driven from the pack to live out his life alone. Without the support of the rest of the pack, it wouldn't be long before he would die. Lucky for the old dogs, they do live with humans, and we watch out for them physically and mentally. Never leave the dogs that are in conflict together unsupervised during this time. The oldest alpha should only play with the smallest, nonthreatening dogs until the power struggle is worked out.

Often, the addition of a young dog can rejuvenate an older dog. But when selecting a companion for your dog, you should keep in mind the personalities of those involved. The selection of a younger friend for a senior should enhance his golden years, not make them torture. You might want to consider adding another older dog for companionship.

My friends Deborah and Harrison did just that. They had to have their beloved dog Luca euthanized at 16 years of age, which left their other older dog, Thanksgiving, as a single dog. After a period of grieving, they were ready for another dog and adopted a wonderful Lab/Rottweiller mix, named Ranger, from the local shelter where Deborah volunteers. Ranger is 4 years old and was surrendered to the shelter because his family was moving.

Thanksgiving and Ranger got along fine, but Deborah and Harrison discovered Ranger required a lot more exercise than Thanksgiving. As a result, Thanksgiving was being left home alone because she was unable to keep up on walks. They felt bad about that situation, so when a 7-year-old Basset Hound was surrendered to the shelter, Deborah got the idea that Buster might round out their canine family perfectly. While getting to know Buster at the shelter, Deborah discovered that he had five owners so far in his life. He seemed like a nice dog, and after Harrison confessed that he had had always considered Basset Hounds to be interesting dogs, Buster joined their family. At last, Buster has a permanent home, and it has worked out great.

Now, when Deborah and Harrison are out walking Ranger, Buster and Thanksgiving stay home and see who can get to Ranger's bed first. Ranger and Buster have also developed a relationship that involves racing around the yard and general roughhousing. The addition of an older dog in this family has benefited all concerned, so be sure to consider all angles when deciding between a puppy or a middle-aged or an older dog.

LOOKING AFTER THE "OLDS"

When your multiple-dog family has dogs of all ages for the most part the younger dogs will respect the older dog. You might have to watch things when you are letting the dogs outside, so the senior doesn't get bowled over in the excitement. Also going up and down stairs can be hazardous for those not as agile as they used to be. You may need to make some adaptions around the house, such as these:

- Lower the dog door to make it easier for the dog to hop in or out.
- Make a ramp to favorite places on the furniture.
- Create a special place for the older dog, away from the rough-housing youngsters (human and canine).
  - Set aside a chair for seniors only.
  - Give the senior a beanbag chair in a quiet, warm corner of the basement.
  - Give your senior permission to sleep on the bed (at long last.)
  - Create a comfortable place by a window where the senior can keep an eye on the neighborhood.
  - Use a baby gate to keep your senior out of harm's way.
  - Build an extra fenced area, so the senior can have some peaceful time outdoors.
- Provide an additional source of heat (but be careful of electrical cords).

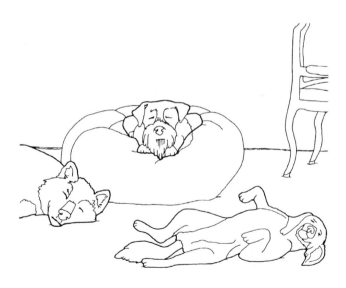

Keep in mind that your older dog probably doesn't see or hear as well as he used to. When you are approaching your sleeping senior, call out his name or stamp your feet to avoid startling him. Check behind your motor vehicles when backing up; it would be horrible to run over your own dog. If your senior's eyesight is failing, you should avoid moving your furniture around. Be careful about letting your older dog outside unattended as he may wander off and not be able to find his way home. You would be shocked how many older dogs end up in shelters. They wander away from home, and the owners think they wandered off somewhere to die, when they are in reality at the shelter.

An older dog may need to wear a sweater or jacket to ward off chills, indoors and out. If your dog is not used to wearing a jacket, it can take some adjustment. Whenever the jacket goes on, make it a big deal with lots of praise and maybe a few food treats. It won't be long before wearing the jacket will make your dog feel special and warm.

An older dog should be fed a high-quality senior dog food. Remember, an overweight dog will have a shorter life, so don't overfeed your older dogs. They are exercising less, so they should eat less than when they were younger (just like us!). You might try moistening the food of your older dog, especially if he has problems with his teeth or gums. You might also find your older dog does better with three or four small meals a day, rather than one or two bigger ones. Another good suggestion for the older dogs in your family is to feed them on an elevated platform, so they don't have to bend down to eat. An upside-down milk crate might do the trick.

OOPS, SORRY MOM

It is not a crime to get older. Thank goodness because I'm not getting any younger either! Our dogs have loved and protected us without reservation. As they age, we often have to make adjustments. One of them might be dealing with an incontinent older dog. This can be a frustrating problem. Of course, a trip to your veterinarian will assure you it is not a medical problem. If your climate is mild, your older dog could spend more time outdoors with a dog house when you are not home to monitor him. When you are home and your dog is inside, you can put an old shower curtain under your dog's washable bedding.

As my old girl Annie (she is 15 years old now) ages, I have discovered I need to let her out more often, a simple solution that I was overlooking. She is not an outdoor-type dog, and there are times I would like to confine her. Since she was never crate trained, she becomes extremely stressed in a crate, so that solution did not work for her. When we are going to be gone for a few hours, I make sure she goes outside before we go. If it is going to be longer than a few hours, I have someone come by and let her out, or I take her with me; she still loves to go for a ride in the car.

Annie has always slept in our bedroom at night on a pillow under the bed. As she has gotten older, she has started leaving the room and urinating in a few carefully chosen spots around the house. We started keeping the bedroom door closed, but I was uncomfortable with that. I never felt I could really hear the kids well enough with the door closed. Then we decided to leash her to the dresser, where she could still get to her spot under the bed. She did not like that, and after a few weeks, she started refusing to come upstairs to bed. She elected to stay in her bed in the family room, which is secured with gates. I miss her upstairs, but she is happy to stay downstairs by the woodstove, and she seems to be able to wait until we get up in the morning to do her business with this arrangement. Since she can wait while she is downstairs, she should be able to wait while she is upstairs, but I guess she chooses not to – go figure.

SAYING GOODBYE

If you are one of the few lucky ones whose dogs age gracefully and die at home, count your blessings. Most dog owners have to make the decision themselves about having their old friends euthanized. This is a heartbreaking decision. The criteria for the decision seems to be the same for almost every one of the respondents:

- Incurable pain and discomfort.
- Loss of a quality life.

You will know in your heart when the time is right, so don't feel pressured by others.

From the responses to the questionnaire, I discovered that this single event in the life of your dog can cause unforgettable regret for the dogs' owners. If you need to have your dog euthanized by injection at your veterinarian's, you have three choices. There may be others, but these are the most common practices.

- You can bring your dog to the veterinarian and leave the dog there for the doctor to euthanize after you go.
- Along those same lines, you can bring the dog to your veterinarian but stay with the dog while he is being injected.
- You can have your veterinarian come to the house and have the injection administered there.

The first choice seems to bring about the most regrets, with people years later still experiencing remorse about that choice. When you leave the body with your veterinarian for disposal, the staff will handle the arrangements. Before you need this service, you should ask what your veterinarian does with the body after the death. The two most common methods of dealing with the remains are group cremations or rendering. The bodies are generally frozen until they can be picked up, usually once a week, and be either brought to a crematorium or sent to a rendering service. A rendering service boils the remains to be used for other products such as wax or fertilizer. Although this may seem distasteful, it is inexpensive, and when money is an issue or you have nowhere to bury a body yourself, it may be the way to go.

Staying with your dog during the last moments in his life seems to bring more satisfaction to most respondents. If you have never been with an animal as it has been euthanized you might not know what to think about the process. It takes very little time and is not painful for your friend. The doctor may or may not shave a spot on the dog's leg where the injection will be given. Depending on the size of the dog, he may be on the table or the floor may be more comfortable. While the doctor is preparing the shot, you will have chance to help your dog feel more comfortable, kiss and hug him, and assure him all dogs in the Great Beyond are young, healthy, and in no pain. Once the injection has been given, your dog will die within moments, very peacefully.

When my husband's Labrador, Alf, was euthanized, he was in extreme pain, and as I saw him lying peacefully on the floor, it was the first time in months the pain was gone. My husband was emotionally unable to take Alf to the veterinarian and be with him, so I took him. It was not an easy time for anyone, but I know John was comforted that I was with Alf as his life ended.

John had just retired from twenty years in the Navy, and I was just starting to work on this book, so money was an issue for us. It was winter, so digging a big deep hole was not an option. The group cremation cost about twice as much as the rendering. We chose the rendering because of money. I brought Alf's collar home and planted a rhododendron in his memory; I care for it as if he were buried under it.

Alf was the alpha dog in our pack. His death left a very empty spot in all of our lives. Our Golden Retriever, Gentry, respected Alf completely, and after Alf was gone for about two weeks, we noticed Gentry's muzzle had turned gray. The loss affected him greatly, and even though we have five dogs, there is not a leader among them. All of our pets, the cat included, went through a period of grief. I felt that they all must have wondered what happened to the canine boss.

The next time we experience a loss, I think I'm going to try the method Susan uses when she has to have her dogs euthanized. Susan always brings the deceased dog home and lays it in the yard, so the other dogs can say their good-byes and not mope and become depressed looking for their pack member. An animal psy chologist shared this idea with her, and it has prevented problems because the dogs are not still waiting for the deceased dog's return. They know where he is.

If your veterinarian will make a house call for this procedure, I think that is the best. Your companion can die in familiar surroundings with his family, canine and human, around.

DISPOSITION ARRANGEMENTS

As I read the responses, I was overwhelmed by the love and tenderness the respondents displayed as they described the funeral arrangements they used for their animals. We all know our dogs will die, so it is best if we have a plan before they leave us. To make arrangements that will be meaningful, with no regrets, you really need to plan ahead. To help you with the plans, I am going to describe the methods used by other dog owners.

In many areas of the country, it is illegal to bury the body of your deceased animal in your yard. If you live in an area where you can bury your animal friends in your backyard, consider that option. It is the least expensive option. A lot depends on the size of the dog and the area of the country where you live. A large dog and rocky terrain will make it difficult to dig a large and deep enough hole. Also, climate is a factor; if the ground is frozen, digging a hole might be impossible. In rural areas you should be concerned about wildlife digging up the buried animal.

You will have to decide what you are going to bury the body in. Here are some suggestions:

- Purchase a coffin.
- Build a box yourself.
- Use a cardboard box.
- Use a piece of luggage.
- Wrap the dog in a blanket.
- Wrap the dog in a plastic bag.

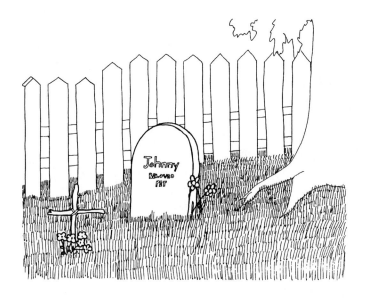

Then, if you like, you can include with the body some of your dog's favorite toys. A backyard burial can be a lovely memorial to your dog. As a multiple-dog owner, you will eventually have a little pet cemetery of your own. The problem is, if you move, you have to leave them all behind, which can be hard. One family moved into a house and discovered markers for an already established pet cemetery. They fixed it up, put a little fence around it, and are continuing to use this special place for their deceased pets.

If it is not practical or if it is illegal for you to bury the body, you might consider cremation. This service is arranged through your veterinarian for the most part, but it depends on the size of the community in which you live. In some smaller communities, your local funeral home or crematorium might be able to arrange the cremation. In some larger cities, this can done through a pet cemetery or a service that caters to pets. Check the phone book, follow through on references, and ask your friends for suggestions to help you find a service that has a good reputation.

You can have a private cremation for your dog and keep the

ashes. The other choice is group cremation. In that case you do not get the ashes back. Every person has different needs. Some people need to have a physical reminder of their pet, such as a burial site or an urn of ashes. Other folks are content with the memory, because they have little attachment to the body once the spirit or soul is gone. Here are some other ideas for those who don't need a body, but would like a special memory:

- Make a donation to a shelter or veterinary school in the name of your deceased dog.
- Plant a tree in your yard as a memorial.
- Donate the body to a veterinary school.
- Hang photographs of deceased pets on a specific wall to make it "the pet wall."

If you need a memorial, here are some ideas for after you have buried the body or ashes:

- Build a planter out of wood or stone above the grave in which to plant flowers.
- Place a marker, which you have made or bought, above the grave.
- Place fresh flowers on the grave regularly.
- Make the area around the grave site a wild bird sanctuary with feeders and a bird bath.

One of the advantages of cremation and keeping the ashes in urns is that when you move you will be able to take the deceased with you. If you choose cremation and keep the ashes, here are some suggestions for that:

- Keep the ashes in a pretty tin or urn in a special area of the house.
- Arrange to have the ashes buried with you when your time comes. [Note: This is an idea that was mentioned many times by respondents. In many states, however, it is illegal to bury

animal remains in human cemeteries. If this is your plan, call a local mortuary to check on any restrictions in your state.]

• Sprinkle some of the ashes in your dog's favorite place outdoors, and save some to bury or keep in an urn.

Another option is a pet cemetery. Pet cemeteries have come under scrutiny in recent years and can be quite costly. For starters, you have the cost of the plot; then every added service has an additional fee. It could easily add up to $500 or more. If this is the option you choose, do your leg work, check references, and ask if the cemetery is a member of the International Association of Pet Cemeteries. This association has set standards and regulations for cemeteries that are members. One such regulation is a guarantee that the ground will never be used for anything other than a burial ground.

Another way to look after your pets is to be sure to include them in your will. You will need to ask a friend or relative to take over guardianship of your pets and to make sure that they have proper care until new homes can be found for them. A sum of cash should be left to the guardian to help with the expenses of caring for your dogs. Some people declare that they would like their dogs killed in the event of their death. This seems like a very selfish way to handle your own death. Dogs are very adaptable and should be able to live out their lives with a new family, not have to die along with you.

THERE YOU HAVE IT

Living with multiple dogs is a joy and challenge, and it can be heart-breaking. From the moment you decide to become a multiple-dog owner to the day you lose the last of your long-time companions, and every moment in between, nothing is more rewarding than owning dogs. I can never imagine my life without dogs.

SUGGESTED READING

Sife. *Loss of a Pet*. Howell Book House, New York, N.Y. 1993

Wilcox and Walkowicz. *Old Dogs, Old Friends, Enjoying Your Older Dog*. Howell Book House, New York, NY. 1991

Bibliography

Arden, Darlene. "Choosing a Veterinarian." *Dog World* July 1992: 36-39

Blevins, Donna Caton. "Finding the Right Resort for Rover." *Dog World* July 1993: 16-18

— "Dog Houses: To Build or to Buy?" *Dog World* September 1993: 38-39.

Brennan, D.V.M., Mary L. *The Natural Dog*. PLUME, New York, New York. 1994

Burnham, Patricia Gail. "Engineering Solutions to Old-Age Incontinence" *Dog World* March 1990: 36-38

Campbell, William E. *Behavior Problems in Dogs*. American Veterinary Publications, Inc. Santa Barbara, CA. 1985

Cargill MA, MBA, MS, John. "Feed That Dog! Part 1" *Dog World* July 1993: 24-29

— "Feed That Dog! Part II" *Dog World* August 1993: 10-16

— "Feed That Dog! Part III" *Dog World* September 1993: 14-22

— "Feed That Dog! Part IV" *Dog World* October 1993: 36-42

Carlson and Giffin. *Dog Owner's Home Veterinary Handbook*. Howell Book House, New York, NY. 1980

Gearhart DVM, Martha S. "Preventing and Treating Lyme Disease." *Dog World* June 1993: 24-34

Mech, L.D. *The Way of the Wolf,* Voyageur Press, MN. 1991

Palika, Liz. "A Holistic Approach" *Dog Fancy* May 1992: 16-17

— "Come, Fido!" Doral Publishing, Wilsonville, OR. 1993

— "Flyball" *Dog Fancy* August 1990: 32-36

Reidarson DVM, Thomas H. "Bloat" *Dog Fancy* June 1990: 33-36

Shaw, Fran Pennock. "Have Dog Will Travel." *Dog World* July 1993: 38-40

Shojai, Amy D. "Heartworm Disease: The Mosquito Menace" *Dog World* July 1993: 32-38

Son, R. Randal. "Skijoring: Peace and Panic" *Dog World* December 1992: 44-45

Stover, T. Mark. Ph.D., Animal Behaviorist, Personal Interview. Seattle, WA. October 15, 1993

Uridel, Faith A. "Alternative Therapies" *Dog Fancy* March 1992: 40-46